Michael Schumacher
Driving Force

Photographs by Michel Comte

Words by Sabine Kehm

Ebury Press

Prologue

'Anyone who becomes a public figure cannot expect leniency, nor demand any.'
Marie von Ebner-Eschenbach

When Michael Schumacher became a public figure, he didn't expect leniency, nor did he demand any. He simply wasn't aware that one day he might be in need of some. But then he didn't know what he was in for...

Michael's first test with a Formula One car was at Silverstone in August 1991. It was far from certain whether this inexperienced youngster could master the Jordan well enough to be allowed to drive in the upcoming race at Spa. Michael drove the car out of the pits and, within a few metres, decided he might as well just switch off the fiendish machine right away. The car was too complex and too powerful.

But he tried a lap and after that one circuit he began to drive as fast as he felt the car was able to manage. That day he drove 36 test laps and in the process he beat Jordan's lap record at Silverstone.

Eleven years later nothing — and everything — had changed. He was still breaking records — just bigger ones. In 2002, Michael won the Formula One World Championship title for the fifth time, emulating the legendary Juan-Manuel Fangio in the 1950s, an achievement which no one thought would ever be repeated. By the end of the 2002 season, he had won a total of 64 Formula One races, more than any other driver in the 50-year history of the sport. And there was no reason to believe that he wouldn't win even more. He has won more races in a season than any other driver, as well as more World Championship points.

No one drives like him — so spectacularly, so safely, so cold-bloodedly, so precisely, so immaculately, and yet with so much enjoyment.

They say he is a legend in his own lifetime. A phenomenon. A kind of extra-terrestrial superhero, never letting up in his urge to battle it out, to duel, to win. They call him names: Rain God. King of the Road. The Master. Schuminator.

A champion. For many, the greatest ever.

As for Michael, he is not sure what to make of all this. The man simply likes driving. It gives him almost boundless pleasure. He enjoys taking the car to its limits on corners and fighting the g-force. The only thing he has ever wanted to do is to race, four wheels around him, in a duel with one of his great rivals. He loves competition. He is the racing driver supreme, passionately dedicated to his sport.

A *racer* is what he is called in England. This is a title he can understand.

Sabine Kehm
February 2003

The Racer: A Dramatic Career

His head felt congested. Heavy eyes, runny nose and husky voice, almost too deep for a 22 year old. The young Formula 3000 driver had arrived at the youth hostel fighting off a heavy cold. It was the end of August 1991, the night before his first weekend of racing in Formula One. He was not well, though he would never show it. Gritting his teeth, he got on with the job in hand.

'I felt rotten. I was ill with a bad cold, something I often had due to the regular long-haul flights to and from Japan. I knew that this wasn't the best state to be in with the weekend of the race coming up. And I wasn't sleeping well either. It wasn't because of the race itself, but because I had been driving Formula 3000 in Japan, and jet-lag was waking me up in the middle of the night. When I arrived that evening in Spa, I felt weirdly restricted. I had that sense of tunnel vision, when you are only aware of those essential things you have to concentrate on.'

One would assume that such days would be engraved on the memory, leaving impressions which would last forever but Michael's memory of that crucial weekend is unusually patchy. They arrived at the youth hostel in the dark and spent the night tossing and turning on camp beds. He remembers there were strange tiles on the walls, 'just like in a school'. The atmosphere was cold and unwelcoming. 'Everything was a funny greeny-blue.' Michael doesn't even remember that he slept in the same room as his manager, Willi Weber. It demonstrates how Schumacher functions, how he functioned even then: never bother with trivialities, or unimportant details, only the essentials count. You have to focus on them, with all the strength at your disposal.

It was pure coincidence that Spa-Francorchamps would be Michael Schumacher's first race. Eddie Jordan urgently needed a driver for his up-and-coming team because his official driver, Bertrand Gachot, had suddenly found himself in jail after an altercation with a London taxi driver. Schumacher was summonsed thanks to his manager Willi Weber, the man with whom he shared the room that weekend in the youth hostel, the man who had given him a drive in his Formula Three team, the man who has subsequently guided Michael's career with such care and foresight, constantly pestering Eddie Jordan. The situation was helped by the fact that Michael's other patron, Jochen Neerpasch, was able to bring to bear the illustrious name of Mercedes. But as much as anything else it was the result of the impression made by the young Formula 3000 driver in testing at Silverstone.

Looking back, however, many Formula One fans regard the fact that Spa was Michael 's first race as anything but coincidence. They see it as somehow predestined, because Schumacher immediately felt himself completely at home on the impressive Ardennes circuit, and because it seems as if this circuit and Michael's Formula One career are intertwined in some indefinable way, as if his life as a racing driver revolves round the enormous corners of this track which he loves so much. In Spa he has experienced glittering highpoints, as well as nerve-shattering crises.

'This circuit is something very special, it has a character all its own. It is a real challenge for every driver, it demands every ounce of your ability. It is far and away my favourite circuit.' Michael is not easily impressed, but when he is talking about the one time Spa-Francorchamps Grand Prix Spa, he becomes lyrical and his eyes brighten.

Perhaps Michael's devotion to Spa stemmed from the fact that he gained his first impressions of the circuit on a bicycle. You get a much more immediate and physical sense of its tremendous difficulty on a bicycle. Never to have driven a circuit like this before is a real competitive disadvantage, and the crafty Weber had assured Jordan that the difficult circuit was indeed a part of his protégé's repertoire — a little white lie.

'There was a story that Willi was asked if I knew the Spa track, and he said that I had already driven it, which wasn't true. Luckily, they only asked Willi. *I just kept quiet and said nothing,*' Michael laughs. So he went and pedalled round the whole hilly track on his bike, and fell in love with it. 'The first corner is not particularly demanding, in a car you brake at about 80 metres, the track is a bit bumpy and drops away to the inside a little at the end, which is why it's easy to lock the right front wheel. And then it's downhill for a while, and I still remember how incredibly surprised I was at its steepness. When you see a track on the TV screen, you don't get a proper impression, especially in Spa, of how hilly it is. Approaching Eau Rouge, it is phenomenal how the angle changes from the entry to the exit. It's mainly Eau Rouge that makes Spa so special. That hollow is a bit like driving up a wall. It climbs and slopes, uphill and down dale. It's totally unique, and very demanding. The only similar experience is Suzuka, and parts of the Nürburgring, but there the corners are too flowing and wide. If you don't get your line right at Eau Rouge, or are too slow, you're scuppered.

'Or take Suzuka where there are a number of S-bends and if you get it right, you can make up a lot of time. On one Suzuka corner, the 130 R, you get a speed reading at the exit and once I clocked 306 kilometres an hour. Moments like that are absolutely tremendous. These high-speed corners make enormous demands on you, but if you get it right, it's a fantastic kick. On the S-bends, you get into a rhythm and feel as if you are really flying. With the speedometer registering an extreme speed you get the sense that you have almost achieved perfection. To drive into one of the ordinary chicanes, braking and then driving through is nothing special because there is hardly anything you can do wrong. Perhaps one of your wheels could stick, and then you could lose control of your steering, but it's the high-speed corners which are the test. They are spectacular and you experience extreme lateral-G force. You have to brake and keep the car under control and you're driving the whole time at the limit.

'Race driving is not a test of courage or a feat of strength. You have to be able to tell whether the car can take a particular corner at a particular speed or not. It is up to you to know how you take this corner but if you need courage to do it, you have a problem. It's about knowing where the limits lie. And Spa is unique in this respect because it has combinations of demanding corners, which require a particular kind of skill. And the landscape in which it is located is unbelievably beautiful.'

It was the first practice session, on that Friday before Michael's Formula One debut. He was standing on the lorry in which the screws and spare parts are stored, right at the back and a long way from the door. Angular face, keeping his thoughts to himself. With a determined look, he slipped the fireproof vest rapidly over his head, pulled up the green overall, put his arms into the sleeves, and did up the zip. On the collar flap, the name of fellow team-mate de Cesaris had been covered over with masking tape, and Schumacher's name written on it. There was no money for an overall of his own, and anyway who knew how long this driver would be in the team? Slowly and carefully Michael folded the end of one collar flap over the other. The overall was a bit too big, a bit too baggy, but who cared. *Cut out what's unimportant, concentrate on the essentials.* Michael looked up briefly at the roof of the lorry and took a deep breath. Then he straightened up and walked with rapid strides across to the garage.

By the end of the weekend's racing the experts had a new name to conjure with — Michael Schumacher. He was clearly someone to watch; a driver who was going places.

He had come through the weekend of the race as if to confirm his manager's statement that he had often been round the Belgian circuit. It was a hint of what was to come. In his first Formula One qualifying session ever, the unknown youngster sensationally fought his way to eighth place, springing a major surprise at the dangerous Blanchimont corner.

'We worked hard on the tuning of the Jordan so that I was able to take Blanchimont at full throttle. That gained us valuable time. You can do that with Formula One cars today but it wasn't always possible then.'

And with this daring stroke Michael won himself the attention of the established drivers. On Sunday the race itself was over for him after only 500 metres due to a damaged clutch.

'I had a very good start and immediately moved up to fifth or so, and wondered why it was all so simple, and why the others all braked so early. As a result I was nearly the cause of the first accident, a frightening moment at the first corner which immediately cost me another place. But then straight after, it was finished: a big disappointment.'

Talking today about 25 August 1991, Michael is not particularly nostalgic. Any such feelings are outweighed by his disappointment at having to drop out so early. His nostalgia is reserved for another moment, just a week before, when he sat for the first time in one of the world's most powerful cars on his first test day as a Formula One pilot.

'When we drove over to the track for the first test drive I had a rather funny feeling in my stomach,' Willi Weber recalls. Michael felt much the same. 'When I got into the car for the first time at Silverstone, that was the really special moment. Much more so than the race at Spa, when I just turned up and drove. That was nothing much to speak of. But the test beforehand was an incredible experience, and a much greater challenge. It was much tougher because I had absolutely no idea at that point what the future held for me, and how I would cope. I can remember the first three laps very clearly. On the first lap I thought: *oops, there goes your Formula One career, it's over*. The car was incredibly impressive, so powerful, and at the same time difficult to drive. On the second lap, I was thinking, *Well, not bad*, but still had somewhat mixed feelings. But then by the third, I was really comfortable with the car. I had a feel for it, saw I was getting the hang of things, and that driving it wasn't beyond me. It seemed that everything was OK but I couldn't be one hundred per cent certain because none of the other Jordan drivers had tested, just two from Arrows, and we only had the times from some earlier tests as points of reference. And I was on used tyres, not new ones. I can't remember precisely what the times were, 1.55, more or less the same as the others, but because I was on used tyres, that was fine.'

After the first three laps on the south circuit, Michael did a further 33 laps that day, setting the lap record for Jordan at Silverstone, previously held by the established driver Andrea de Cesaris. His calmness and outstanding adaptability were strikingly apparent even on this first test drive. In 1991, unlike today, it was a gigantic step from Formula 3000 to Formula One. It was a matter of driving completely different cars, the grip was so much greater than in the smaller class, the deceleration much more fierce and the acceleration more intense. Everything was so much faster, but Michael made the switch quickly and easily. Even the fact that he had to test drive with chassis 191 — the one he was due to drive in the grand prix a few days later — and that a crash would have meant the end of his big chance, didn't cause him to drive with exaggerated care. And he began as he meant to go on, by breaking a record. He was in his element.

'At first you think how fabulous this is, how fabulous the people are, and what an incredible point in your life this is going to be, what a great step. Jordan was a great team to be working with. But then everything very quickly got back to normal.'

It is significant that when Michael looks back, he often talks of his next race, at Monza, as his first Formula One race: 'The first time I raced, I never had any idea that I would make it so far. That was in Monza in 1991 when I drove further than 500 metres for the first time. I got into a wheel to wheel with the great Ayrton Senna because he was having difficulties right at the beginning of the race, and I was able to chase and attack him, even though I couldn't find a way to overtake. That was the moment I realised that we all only cook with water. If someone is sitting in the right car at the right time, they can beat anyone. I realised that then, and still believe it today.'

The test drive at Silverstone, the race at Spa, and then the abrupt change of team. The experts were astonished. In the next race at Monza in November 1991, Michael was already wearing a yellow overall, and this one had his own name on it. Within those two weeks, his life had completely changed.

'Switching to Benetton was my big chance for the future. We knew at that time that Jordan was going to get Yamaha engines, and we felt that this would be catastrophic. And when this chance came up, we grabbed it. It wasn't exactly pleasant, driving barely 500 metres for the team which had given me the opportunity to get started, and then to immediately drop them. But that was what I had to do at the time.'

One year later, 1992, back in Spa and it was raining. Typical Ardennes weather, overcast, changeable, damp and foggy. Fans worldwide will come to call this 'Schumi weather', because no one drives with such reliable instinct under these conditions. Formula One cars have no windscreen, there's just a visor to protect the driver's eyes, and this often mists over. In the rain, vision is down to virtually nil, spray blurs the contour of the cars almost completely, and driving becomes a mixture of experience, touch, and trusting that your fellow competitors will drive sensibly. Michael had been a Formula One driver for a year. He achieved his first podium place at the beginning of the 1992 season in Mexico, and he knew that he could hold his own going for a win.

The slip-up occurred in lap 30. Lying in third place and approaching Stavelot, Michael was battling with team-mate Martin Brundle, when he slid off into the gravel trap. Brundle overtook him. Michael was lucky, he recovered from the spin and got back on the track. But sitting behind Brundle, he noticed that his tyres were completely worn, and knew that he had to get into the pits straightaway. Both cars had been prepared identically for the race, and as a consequence the tyres on both would have undergone the same wear and tear. A rapid radio message to the pit wall: 'I'm coming in for a tyre change.' While the rest of the drivers were struggling to cope with the conditions, and skidding about on the wet track, Schumacher made his way to the pits and had rain tyres fitted. Just this one lap on the right tyres gave him a decisive advantage over his rivals.

A few hours later, it's still raining and the man who, over the years to come, will be up there more often than any other driver before, stood on the podium for the first time. 'Of course it's nice to think back to that first victory. It was a rather curious business, because I won as a result of an error. It was obvious that my tyres would be in the same condition as Martin's, and the thought shot through my mind: *I've got to get to the pits immediately.* The decision was worth its weight in gold, because under those conditions the tyre change gave me a five-second lead, and to that extent my team-mate helped me to achieve the win, for which I am very grateful. It was a great feeling to be on the podium, and it took a long time to sink in.' If they had not already realised, the established drivers now knew that they had a serious rival to contend with.

German racing fans had had to wait 17 long years for a victory by a German driver. Jochen Mass had won in 1975 in Spain, under tragic circumstances after an accident in which Rolf Stommelen was badly injured and five spectators and a fire marshall were killed. Schumacher dedicated his win to the fans. He was overjoyed at the time, but in retrospect is surprised at his emotions: 'Looking back, I wouldn't say that it was my finest victory. I really enjoyed those moments when they were happening, but afterwards I wanted to move on to the next challenge. That's the way things functioned then, but my reactions aren't so extreme now. When I became World Champion for the fifth time in 2002 at Magny Cours, I was much more moved than I was in Spa a decade earlier. I've no idea why, perhaps it's down to age. Perhaps these things have a different value later in life. And besides, one win is one thing, but five championships is much more.

'I think another factor is that when I first came in to Formula One, I didn't really understand what it was all about. I could drive fast, of course, but I had little idea about the complexity of the whole business, which little wheel you had to set in motion in order to get everything going. At that time I was a greenhorn. Over the years, you grow into it much more, feel yourself much more of a link in the chain. In effect, I just used to drive. It's true that the engineers would listen to my views, but they didn't know how they were supposed to evaluate them. Things are certainly different today, and that's why I feel differently, feel I am much more a part of things, and consequently get much more satisfaction from the victories. From certain little gestures, I can see what the engineers are thinking, how they are weighing up what I have to say, what value they attach to it. And that's why I am much more emotional today than I used to be, because I am much more involved — at least that is one of the reasons for it.'

Year on year Michael has always produced something special at Spa. It's where he grew to be a star, and where some of the most extraordinary elements of the Schumacher legend occurred.

Take 1994, for instance, when he was on the way to his first World Championship. Most reporters had already left to go home, the news of Michael's most recent victory in Belgium was already in print when, late that evening, came the news from the World Motor Sports Council that Michael was to be disqualified because of a breach of the 10mm minimum clearance regulations for the underside of the car. The lower panel had been worn down below the allowed limit.

'I made a stupid mistake at the chicane combination. I drove too wide leaving the left-hand corner, the rear wheel hit the dirt, and the car spun off the course. But I was quite lucky. I was going so fast, the car swung round through 360 degrees and I was able to carry on. But on the spin I clattered over the kerb and ruined the skid block. This led to the much discussed disqualification. I can almost laugh about it today, because ultimately everything turned out fine.' But it was no laughing matter at the time.

This was one of the significant events of Michael's career. Due to the gearbox problem and changeable weather, he had only managed 16th place in qualifying and his rival Damon Hill was in 8th. After the first lap, Hill was 6th, Michael 13th, and a lap later they were 5th and 10th respectively. By the third lap Hill was in 5th and Michael was 8th. On lap 14 Hill was in the lead and Michael was in 3rd. One lap later Hill and Berger went into the pits before him and Michael was at the head of the field. In 15 laps he had fought his way from 16th at the start to first. Three laps later he went into the pits and then the rain came. Hill changed to rain tyres. Michael didn't. Despite frequent demands from his race engineer, Pat Symonds, to change to rain tyres, he kept ahead of Damon Hill in the rain on his slicks.

'That was a real ding-dong battle with Damon. He was actually faster than me, we were driving on different tyres in mixed conditions, and, as the saying goes, somehow my car was wider than his . At any rate, I made it difficult for him to pass. On the section coming up to Blanchimont you're at full throttle, but there are corners, and you can choose your line so as to make things difficult for your opponent. I remember there was quite a lot of discussion at the time. Damon wasn't entirely in agreement with the line I took. Personally, I thought it was really rather good.'

The young up-and-coming driver had found himself at the centre of an extremely controversial season, the repercussions of which continue to rumble on even today. Following Spa he was in an alarming situation — although he had had a good start to the season, his lead in the World Championship was under threat. This was meant to be the breakthrough season, the first challenge for the World Championship title, but it was overshadowed by a number of inconsistencies and irregularities. Much more seriously the season saw the deaths of Ayrton Senna and Roland Ratzenberger.

'Schummi the cheat' stuck to Michael in the way rubber sticks to tarmac. There were constant whispers from his opponents about breaches of regulations by the World Championship leader's team. Constant questions and endless wrangling, sometimes with the World Motor Sports Council. Rumours about a banned traction control, the ignored black flag at Silverstone for which Michael received a two-race ban, the faulty refuelling jig at Hockenheim. These reports repeatedly overshadowed Schumacher's performances behind the wheel. He achieved second place in Barcelona with the car stuck in fifth gear for almost the whole race and his victory in the rain at Spa was further testimony to his immaculate touch.

Not until the very last race of the 1994 season would the World Championship title be decided. Against this dramatic backdrop, Michael and Damon were to clash yet again. After Silverstone, Michael had received a two-race ban for ignoring a black flag, and, in addition, the points for that race and the race at Spa were deducted, in effect losing him the points from four races. Adelaide was to be the climax and Michael had just a one-point advantage over Damon.

Lap 36 and Michael suddenly slid off on to the grass and into the wall. Either some part of his front suspension was damaged or his tyres were clogged with mud and grass but as a result controlling his car was difficult. Hill tried to pass on the inside but Michael defended his line and closed the gap, actually driving over Damon's front wheel (an unwritten rule of Formula One is that that the corner belongs to the man in front, and that was clearly Schumacher). Discussions after the race were heated because Schumacher and Hill took opposing views of events.

'Those long minutes standing out on the track, waiting for the outcome were tense. I was completely distraught and didn't know what to do with myself. I didn't know what had happened to Damon, and knew that we both had a big points advantage over the drivers in fourth, fifth and sixth place. And so it wouldn't be a problem for Damon to pick up the one point I had over him. Out there, you don't know what's going on, so I tried to listen to the track commentator. It was difficult because I could only hear snatches of what he was saying, the rest was drowned out by the cars roaring past. I watched out for Damon going past, then I heard something about... "Hill into the pits ... problems ... can he go again"... but he never reappeared. I didn't know what to think, didn't know whether to be pleased or not, my feelings were very mixed. The waiting was awful. A steward came up, stretched out his hand to congratulate me, but I still wasn't sure. When it was finally confirmed, the feeling was indescribable. I was so confused, it was difficult to get things straight. It took a long time to really sink in that I was World Champion.'

In contrast to the preceding season, there was never any dispute in 1995 about the title. 'But even so, by the end of the '95 season I knew I had to move on. I wanted to improve, I needed fresh motivation, and there were two options, one with McLaren, and one with Ferrari. Briefly, there was also an opportunity at Williams, but in the end I decided it came down to the two of them.' An internal dispute meant that Michael's relationship with Benetton Team boss Flavio Briatore was under a cloud. The original contract was due to last until the end of 1996 but was renegotiated to finish at the end of 1995. Many insiders had been hoping that Michael would leave the team which, as a result of the incidents in 1994, was suspected of shady practice.

But Michael's transfer to Ferrari was hardly a straightforward affair and there were to be many difficult years ahead. The alliance with Ferrari was threatening to fall apart . Even within the first 1996 season, a dreadful summer with too many retirements was damaging the reputation of the twice World Champion, and the standing of team boss Jean Todt. A series of technical defects culminated in calls from the Italian media for Todt's dismissal. Yet again the win at Spa in 1996 was to have special significance for Michael. 'I don't know what would have happened had we not won that race,' says Michael, thinking back to his crisis time with the Scuderia. Even Jean Todt bears the 'release' which he felt after the victory at Spa like a scar on his soul. But the great prize eluded them that season: Michael was placed third in the World Championship.

The 1997 season that followed saw the nadir of Michael's career. Everything once again came down to the final race, the European Grand Prix at Jerez. Once again, he had a one-point lead, and this time his opponent in the Williams was Jacques Villeneuve.

On lap 48, and with Michael ahead of the Canadian, there was a collision which would have serious consequences for the German's image and would shroud the race in scandal. When Villeneuve, clearly the faster of the two, suddenly attacked and tried to overtake, Schumacher rammed his Ferrari into the Williams in an act of desperation and slid off ignominiously into the gravel trap. Later accused of making a mistake, he slithered around no less. 'It took me a long time to see what I'd done. I probably didn't want to admit it. At first, I really thought that Jacques was not in front of me, and that it was right to defend my line. And there were a lot of points which confirmed my initial conviction. For instance, we were summoned by the stewards, and they judged that it had been a normal racing incident. Nothing particularly serious, they said, and I thought: *there you go, that's what I thought.*'

But while Michael was having a joke in the tent, chatting to Bernie Ecclestone about skiing and taking a belated lunch with his mechanics and engineers, out in the paddock there was a mounting sense of indignation, which during the course of the next day would swell to a tide of worldwide outrage. Michael was disqualified and Villeneuve was crowned World Champion. Michael felt no sense of guilt, and had completely misread the seriousness of the situation. 'Not until the evening did my misguided conviction about the accident start to fall apart,' he says. 'I remember it exactly, because I was absolutely stunned when our president Luca di Montezemolo said to me something along the lines of "What on earth have you done?" and I thought, *I beg your pardon? How come I'm suddenly the idiot?* He was the first to approach me about it, and in the course of the next few weeks I came to recognise that I was in the wrong, and had made a mistake. Since then I have repeatedly said that if there is one thing I could do over again in Formula One, it would be the race at Jerez in 1997.'

In Jerez, Michael also came into conflict with the changing views about codes of conduct. These changes had come about gradually over the years and he had not taken them on board. Which is why Michael's insight into the incident with Villeneuve was so slow in coming. Michael had grown up with incidents between Senna and other drivers deliberately ramming into each other to stop their rivals from winning the title. In those days, such actions were acknowledged as part of the racing game and the spectators accepted it with a nod and a wink. 'From time to time drivers would even overtake on the parade lap, although officially it was forbidden. But no one paid any attention, it was OK to do it. Perhaps there's a better example in football. Players who took a deliberate dive in the area and got themselves a penalty were regarded in Germany for a long time as being rather smart. Suddenly, they were being slated for it. That's how I felt at first about Jerez.'

In 1998, Spa was once again to be the setting for a sensational event. There were the usual Spa conditions — a lot of rain — and the dramatic course saw a mass pile-up on the first start. Miraculously, no one was hurt. After the second start, it seemed as if Michael, in racing conditions which he could handle better and more sensitively than any other driver, would safely cruise to victory. Then, virtually at full throttle, and in the process of lapping, his Ferrari slammed into the back of David Coulthard's McLaren-Mercedes, just managing to limp to the pits on three wheels, abandoning what would have been a certain win. Incredibly irate, his face contorted with rage, Michael stormed over to the silver pits, and yelled at Coulthard: 'Did you want to kill me?' Nobody had ever seen him so angry, so out of control, so loud. At that moment he was convinced that Coulthard had wanted to cause the accident.

Even now Michael shakes his head in disbelief when he thinks back to the incident. 'I don't know when I was ever so outraged as I was with David that day. But at the time I really thought that he had done it deliberately. No one takes their foot off the pedal in those murky conditions, especially on the straight. David just held his line, and slowed down. I couldn't possibly anticipate that, especially from an experienced driver like him, and particularly given the conditions and all that spray making it impossible to calculate the distance between the cars. That happened to me on another occasion, when I drove into the back of Pedro de la Rosa and on that occasion people believed me when I said you couldn't see a thing.

'I know it's rather difficult to understand, but perhaps it will help if I tell you that it is sometimes a very uncomfortable feeling, particularly in the warm-up lap, if the rain is so heavy you can't see anything in the rear mirror. If I can't see the man behind me, then I know that he can't see me either.

Ross takes off his glasses for the fourth time and painstakingly polishes them. Team boss Jean Todt's wet hair is plastered to his head. Michael's race engineer at the time, Luca Baldisserri, has no hair at all. It has been shaved off, the result of a bet about the World Championship. He is pulling one of the aerodynamicists over to a chair which, in the course of the evening, will see several other members of the team leave with their heads shaven. Michael's wife, Corinna has completely lost track of just who has given her a kiss on the cheek. Michael, certainly, more than once, as he tirelessly cavorts amidst all the excitement.

Soon after the most decisive race weekend of his career, Michael made the following diary entries.

Thursday, 5 October 2000
The question was always the same: 'getting nervous?' I was constantly confronted with it from the moment I arrived in Japan. And the worst of it was, I wasn't at all on edge. Left to myself I was well able to suppress any thoughts about the World Championship. It was just that these questions repeatedly brought the thought back to the surface, and started making me nervous.

We knew that this could be the decisive moment and I remember the race very well — in fact I remember the entire weekend which saw the fulfilment of the dream of the World Championship with Ferrari. It was undeniably a special weekend, the whole season had been geared towards it, although all the team were desperately behaving as if it were a weekend like any other. You have to do this, I believe there is no other way. After the race in Indianapolis I had gone back to Mugello for two solid days of testing. It was quite strenuous, not least because of the time difference, but I was willing to do what was necessary. Because I was absolutely determined to be World Champion.

The testing had gone very well. We even set a new lap record for Mugello and this gave me a feeling of security, for naturally I knew that the chances were good: an eight-point lead is nothing to sniff at. It would, however, have been the biggest mistake ever to have assumed that we had already won. It was clear from seeing what had happened to Mika in Indianapolis how quickly things can change in Formula One. It is never one hundred per cent certain that you won't have to drop out. It could have been on the cards that I would leave Japan two points behind the winner. That's the way I have to approach such matters. It's simply the way I am: always start by being pessimistic.

Immediately after the Ferrari race days in Hockenheim, I had flown with Corinna to Asia to acclimatise as soon as possible to the change in time zone and the different weather conditions. We travelled to a hotel in Thailand, and then on Wednesday on to Suzuka. When we got there we had a good long lie-in. This weekend, of all weekends, I had to be fit.

Friday
I slept so badly — one or two hours at the most. Everyone would say that it's because of the championship, but I don't think so. It wasn't as if my head was so full of thoughts that I couldn't switch off. I think it was more to do with the time change. I have phases where I find it hard to come to terms with it. And then when a lot of things come together — such as the flight back from Indianapolis, the testing and the Ferrari days — it tends to throw you a little off balance and you sleep badly. But I knew I would somehow get back on course.

That day, everyone was talking about the earthquake, which was fine by me. At last there was another topic of conversation, and not the same question again and again — 'are you nervous?' I didn't have much to say about the earthquake because I didn't feel it at all in the car. Corinna was walking along the side of the track during the second practice session and said she didn't feel anything either but it must have been pretty violent in the paddock.

The car was in good fettle from the start. The data from the very promising test of the previous week seemed to be confirmed, although I was honestly not relying on us having six-tenths of a second advantage over the McLarens. A lot of journalists were asking about the times and in Mugello we had been going much faster with the new tyres. Thankfully at Suzuka it was no different.

Everything was going well. The team were incredibly concentrated and you could see they were working calmly. There was a fantastic tautness in the atmosphere which you could almost take hold of. It was a real pleasure to see that everyone was focused on the goal. The briefings were lengthy, because everyone was absolutely determined that there would be no mistakes on Saturday and Sunday.

There was no point driving back to the hotel, so Corinna and I stayed at the track and ate supper with the team. It was already late enough.

Saturday
Another largely sleepless night. But the next day I didn't notice it because I was so focused. Achieving pole position was a first step, though it was extremely close, just nine 10,000ths of a second separated me from Mika. But qualifying was really enjoyable, because Mika and I were goading each other on. Later that afternoon, following all the press conferences, excited rumours were rife, particularly in the press, but they were also being discussed among the team. Ron Dennis had apparently complained that there was an Italian among the Suzuka race stewards. He seemed to be questioning his neutrality. Apparently he had also suggested to certain journalists that we were using traction control and this meant that a possible protest was in the offing. He also seemed to be annoyed by the FIA appeal to the drivers not involved in the battle for the World Championship not to intervene. If it came to the worst, according to the FIA, a driver could be punished. But neither Mika nor I were relying on the help of other drivers, especially our team mates. It was quite clear that we would try from the beginning to take off and drive our own race from the front.

But the rumours went through the paddock like wildfire. I didn't care, I just didn't want to be distracted and I noticed that everyone's concentration was already intensifying. Everyone knew exactly what was at stake. We wanted this title. I wanted to finally win this title.

Once again our briefings were so thorough and lengthy that Corinna and I stayed at the track and had supper with the mechanics and engineers. It was far too late to go anywhere else. And, in any case, I didn't want to. I wanted to be there, with the team. I tend to always do this on the Saturday before the race.

There was a further sleepless night to follow. Those three nights in Suzuka were the most disrupted of my life. Physically, I felt completely shattered, but nevertheless, as soon as I was at the track and in the race, I felt no after-effects at all.

entrance, champagne was being served, and the first members of the team to drift in were a little glassy-eyed.

When you have worked so hard all weekend, a good hotel bed can be very seductive. Michael and Corinna arrive and immediately order some food. 'I need something solid on my stomach if I'm going to celebrate,' laughs Michael. And so they eat Wienerschnitzel with pommes frites, his favourite meal from the go-kart days. Heribert Füngeling, one of Michael's oldest friends from Kerpen, his brother Ralf, and his manager Weber are already whirling around on the dance floor. For someone with the legendary stamina of the World Champion their invitation is irresistible. Someone as fit as him is unlikely to get tired dancing.

In Budapest 2001, Michael refines his sirtaki-dancing technique, and Ferrari's race technical manager Nigel Stepney practises the art of the surprise attack almost to perfection. With a bottle of champagne in hand, he never lacks for victims to attack, drifting across the dance floor like a restless poltergeist, wandering among the tables, and hanging around the buffet with a fat cigar in his mouth — and woebetide anyone who catches his eye. Just as the year before the colour of Michael's shirt changes in the course of the evening from white to dark-blue, and Nigel himself is not spared the champagne shower.

Next morning Michael and Corinna are about to take the lift down to the underground car park. A breathless room maid runs up to reception: has Mr Schumacher already checked out? She has found his passport while cleaning the room. The hotel manager runs down the stairs and catches the Schumachers as they are getting into the car — a not exactly unimportant item if he wants to get back into Switzerland. Corinna smiles to herself. On the way to the airport, a second fright: they take a route which Michael knows well but the road is blocked. The evening before many streets in the inner city have been sealed off for the national holiday. Michael stops the car right in front of the barrier and looks at Corinna. Does she know an alternative route to the airport? Corinna shakes her head, and another car brakes to a halt next to them. It is a camera team which has been following them, and they have a map of the city in the car. 'That was probably the first time that it was an advantage to be pursued by a camera team,' Michael later remarks.

The 2001 season brought the Schumacher-Ferrari alliance their first 'all-time' records. Michael had won more Grand Prix victories than anyone before and Ferrari was acquiring an aura of invincibility which would be consolidated in 2002. The world was bowing in recognition of the team which had won the title in flawless and seemingly effortless fashion. It was also bowing to Michael Schumacher.

Following his win of the 2001 World Championship, Michael gave this interview.

Q: Michael, very many congratulations. Your seventh victory of the season, your 51st overall and your fourth World Championship title. How do you feel?

MS: In the slow-down lap I talked to the team over the radio. As usual, I simply couldn't find the right words. I'm quite a good racing driver, but at such moments I can't express myself properly. Please don't get annoyed at me. I can't say much more. It was a marvellous weekend. We did everything that had to be done. For whatever reason, I came here with a funny feeling. I spoke to Jean and told him I thought we wouldn't do it. But we got pole position, the title, and I got my 51st win, the same number as Alain Prost. This is all just a bit too much for me. I would like to say that this was a great success for us here, on account of the way in which it was achieved. The team Rubens and I have is simply wonderful. I can't describe how, in good times and bad — especially in bad — we stick together. They are a tremendous crew, I love them all, and it's a great pleasure to work with them. This is their success, and I would like to thank them.

Q: How do you see this title, compared to the previous ones?

MS: You are always asking me for comparisons. They are absolutely irrelevant, we just want to enjoy this one. Every title, and every win feels different. Winning a Grand Prix, or even a title, is always a very special feeling.

Q: Michael, your career overlaps with Alain Prost's. Did you admire him when you first came into Formula One, and have you already spoken to him about the record you have set today?

MS: I was with him yesterday in the motor home and he told me to win today so that he no longer has to answer all these irritating questions. He will certainly be very happy now. I probably have to win one more race, we are level at the moment. Naturally, all the big names meant a lot to me when I first started in Formula One, but they were so remote that I never worried myself thinking about outdoing them. I have great admiration for what Alain accomplished, and it makes me very proud to have achieved the same.

Q: What challenges still remain for you in the season?

MS: To win races. After winning the World Championship last year, I said I wanted to win as often as possible. Although I now have the title in my pocket, I want to go on winning, because if things don't go well in the next race, no one will remind me how fantastic it was here in Hungary. They will be drawing my attention to the mistakes I've made instead. That's the way Formula One is. Every race is a fresh challenge for me, and I want to measure up to it. Competing is the fascination. There is still enough fire in my belly to push hard.

Q: This year everything seemed fairly straightforward. Does that make the title less attractive?

MS: Not at all. David Coulthard got it right when he said just now that, if he hadn't had all those problems, he could have fought it out with me right to the last. So I don't feel in the least that I have to put in less effort than I used to. Apart from the first two races, it was always very close and hard-fought.

Q: Do you think you can overtake Juan Manuel Fangio's five titles?

MS: It's not really a goal I have set myself. But in any case, it's a limp comparison since what Fangio achieved at that time in Formula One was simply exceptional. Everything is different today, just from the safety point of view alone. You could never have envisaged then going as fast as we do today. Comparisons are unfair.

Q: How great is your satisfaction at having found the perfect combination of team, car and driver?

MS: Very great. From the beginning, since we have been working together, it has been our aim to arrive at this point. And to be honest, I have the feeling that we still haven't reached the pinnacle of our possibilities. I believe we can achieve even more.

Q: So you think you are not yet in a position of total dominance?

MS: No, certainly not. I believe that there are still some mechanical improvements to be made, and that Ferrari can reach even greater heights.

Q: What's next? What do you still want to achieve?

MS: Simply to continue driving, to continue winning, for as long as possible. We have always said that we want to establish a 'Ferrari era', a particular period in Formula One which is dedicated to Ferrari. We have started on this, and I hope we can maintain it for a good while longer.

2002 saw the fulfilment of the promises of the previous two years. It was also something of a humiliation for the competition, since the Scuderia had started the season with the old car, and won even with that. Ferrari were victorious in 15 out of the season's 17 races. Michael winning 11 of them, making them far and away the best team in Formula One. Even worse for his rivals was that Michael did not have to drop out a single time, and the Scuderia was never really challenged in any of the victories, with the laps after the last pit stop becoming showcases for the team and its sponsors. Red won, red shone, red was once again the colour of Formula One.

By the end of the season Ferrari were being described as invincible, unconquerable and dominant. And in response, fundamental rule changes were introduced into Formula One, widely interpreted by the media as an attempt to put the brakes on Ferrari.

Ferrari and Michael had developed a bond far and away beyond the convenient alliance of the first months of their union. They were now the symbolical incarnation of the Ferrari, symbolic too of the all-in-one transmission package – thought to be the secret of their success and rumours of which were rife in the paddock but which always remained nothing more than rumours. The outstanding characteristics of this relationship were the acceptance, esteem and equality which existed on both sides. A model which probably made the Ferrari era possible — a marriage clearly destined to last for some while yet. The race in Magny Cours which saw Michael become the 'fastest' World Champion of all time — no other driver has ever become World Champion so early in the season — demonstrates the nature of this partnership. It was the product of perfect teamwork, and when it was suggested to Michael after the victory ceremony that he was now a living legend, he dismissed the compliment: 'No, the team is the legend, not me. I couldn't do any of this without them. The fact that we have won the title so early is mainly down to the work of all those people one seldom sees — as well as to the people in the factory in Maranello who work tirelessly for our success. They all have their part in it. And also the team at the circuit, they are all such fantastic people.' People for whom, after three victories, celebrating has become a fine art.

It is 21 July 2002, after the Grand Prix at Magny-Cours. The mechanics, all in their red team clothing, just like last year, and the year before, demand their traditional glass of red wine. It is late when they get back to the Hotel Renaissance where Ferrari are celebrating their victory and Michael's fifth World Championship title. The cars have had to be dismantled and loaded for the journey to Hockenheim for the next race which is only a week away. And so it's nearly midnight before they receive their acclaim. When they arrive through the hedge round the terrace of the Renaissance, they bring a bit of reality to the celebrations which are in full swing. Their trousers are dirty, their shirts covered in oil, confirmation in person that, yes, there was this race, and it was a triumph. Every single one of them is greeted with a standing ovation. They go into the large room inside. And then comes the red wine. A kind of initiation. Everyone is called up, one by one, and has to stand at the head of the first table. They are handed a full glass of red wine and, to the acoustic accompaniment of the mechanics, have to down it in one. And they all do it: Michael. Corinna. Luca di Montezemolo. Jean Todt. Ross Brawn. And in between, the mechanics, one by one.

This year Michael is sporting a beige shirt and smoking a fat cigar. And some time later he appears with a strip of denim tied dashingly round his head. The denim jeans belong to Rubens and unfortunately the left leg is now hanging in tatters. The World Champion has a faraway look in his eye, and at some point ends up behind the bar. The boys are asking for Cuba Libre, and he mixes them one, 'à la Schumi', with constantly changing ingredients. His engineers, Luca, Chris and the others, can in any case no longer tell the difference, and he hands them glass after glass, in between washing up, drying glasses, drawing on his cigar and grinning at Corinna who is plying the boys with gin and tonic. The beige shirt in the meantime has a few more of its buttons undone, and Michael wants to celebrate. Or rather, he insists that others dance by dragging them mercilessly on to the improvised dance floor, ignoring their protestations. Or he leads them in the polonaise. No one is allowed to sit one out, and any flagging is out of the question. The World Champion is tireless, and only the combined forces of Corinna and his manager Willi Weber succeed in getting him out of the hotel and into a taxi. By this time, there is hardly anyone left.

Next morning, at breakfast, even the ever-fit athlete looks a little the worse for wear.

'I have been feeling remarkably relaxed the whole weekend. Largely because I haven't been thinking about the title — somehow I didn't feel that it would happen here. When I saw that Rubens had stopped, and that our pace was easily better than Montoya, I started to believe it was possible. But then I made a mistake. It was my fault — as I was driving out of the pit lane I crossed the white line. I don't know by how much, but it was closer to millimetres than centimetres. But driving over the line is driving over the line and then everything seemed to be lost. What with that drive-through penalty and a few attacks I made on Kimi, the race was extremely eventful. He drove a fantastic race and I don't think I could have found a way past without a tail-ender at the right spot. It seemed it wasn't going to happen.

'Ten laps from the finish I started to pile the pressure on, because you never know what can happen. I don't think it was the pressure from me which provoked Kimi into making an error. It's just that if you don't see the oil, you don't see it, and that's that, regardless of where you brake. Seeing that he had had a problem was a warning for me, and I was able to react in time, which gave me my chance to overtake. And suddenly I did feel that this could be the World Championship. It was simply luck, and I really wasn't expecting it, but things like that happen in motor sport — you have to keep trying right to the very end, and sometimes you'll get your chance.

'I think those were the worst five laps of my career. They seemed to take an eternity. Those are the moments when you suddenly realise how much it all means to you, how much you love this sport, and how determined you are. There was suddenly this weight on my shoulders and the pressure not to make any mistakes, not to get things wrong. Although it's very difficult to be overtaken when you are in front, the pressure was still enormous, and the outburst of feeling was pretty powerful. I've only just realised just what kind of pressure I was probably under. I was so happy that we achieved it together, with an unbelievable team, with people behind me whom I love and admire for their effort, and their commitment and motivation. I have a very close relationship with all the team and it is fantastic to achieve something like this together. Thank you is a very small word for what they have done for me.

'I'm still hungry for more success. I will try to have as many good races as possible, simply because of the pleasure I get from driving. And hopefully that will involve winning another World Championship. Our team is in such good form that I believe we can deliver on this ambition. After all, that's what we live and work for.'

At the end of the 2002 season many complained of boredom. Others observed that we had witnessed the art of motor sport at its highest level. Can perfection ever be boring?

During the 2001 and 2002 seasons Michael and the Ferrari team set two quite special records, and both occurred at Michael's old hunting ground of Spa. In 2001 Michael won his 52nd Grand Prix, thereby overtaking Alain Prost's 51 victories, and taking him to the top of the sport's all-time great list. The circle seemed to be closing. In 2002 he achieved a tenth win in one season, a record which he was later to extend with the victory in Suzuka. But even more important to him was wiping out a minor blemish on his record. In 2002 he secured the first pole position in Spa of his career.

'I was not really aware of it until it was pointed out that I had never been on pole position at Spa, and I was asked whether that bothered me. So I tried to do something about it.' With the pressure off in the battle for the World Championship, the 2002 Belgian Grand Prix became a demonstration not only of Schumacher's sheer ability, but also of the fun and pleasure he gets from driving. Up until his second pit stop, when he consciously restrained himself, he raised the art of driving to its highest level, enrapturing everyone who watched him.

'The reason I feel so much at home here is because it's the track closest to my home town Kerpen, and there are always lots of my fans to support me. But mainly it's the feeling you get here from driving at the very limit, your own physical and mental limits and the absolute limits that the car can bear.'

To have seen Michael at Spa on the weekend of the 2002 Belgian Grand Prix was to watch a driver in his prime, relaxed, confident and relishing the challenge ahead. He seemed to have a gentle smile engraved on his face for days and his walk was more elastic than usual, his bearing even more self-confident. He looked like a man who was savouring every moment and was fully aware of just how well things were going.

On the Friday after the first practice session, Michael was sitting on one of the red boxes in the Ferrari garage, dangling his legs and watching the mechanics at work. The briefing was about to start and the look in Michael's eyes as he gazed at his racing car was one of sheer anticipation. He knew what the car was capable of and the prospect of the challenging Spa track in this impeccable machine filled him with exhilaration. For the first time in his career he was looking at a car in which he could tackle this circuit exactly as he would like.

The weekend duly fulfiled its promise. It turned out to be a fabulously enjoyable driving experience for the man who was already World Champion for the fifth time. His average speed was 225.970 kph. After the first lap he was already 2.2 seconds ahead of his team-mate Rubens Barrichello, who was in an identical car. Between the second and 15th laps he hammered out the fastest lap time for this stretch of tarmac eleven times. Later he said that he was able to 'really let rip' and tried to describe what he meant by being 'close to the limit'. He wouldn't succeed, because none of his listeners was really in a position to know how this could possibly feel. But what became very clear was how much the best racing driver in the world loves his sport, how much he revels in his time at the wheel. The people watching him smiled and shook their heads at the sheer pleasure he still clearly gets from driving after twelve years in the sport. His friend Jean Todt observed that 'He is consumed by a love of driving. He lives in order to race, and when he is in the cockpit he seems to transcend himself. The track is his drug, and he can never get enough of it.'

'What still spurs me on as a Formula One racing driver is essentially my enjoyment of driving. I drove go-karts for 15 years, and am still mad enough to take part in the final of the go-kart World Championship, as I did in 2001, after the end of the Formula One season. So my love of driving — the sheer pleasure of it — is what keeps me motivated and as long as that's still there, I will continue racing.

'That pleasure is the feeling of being on the borderline, of developing one's potential, of constantly pushing back the limits. That's what makes the sport so interesting. Qualifying in 2002 at Suzuka is a good example. Driving a good time there is a fantastic feeling, you really come alive, surpass yourself. I drove 1:32.484. According to our predictions, I should only have driven 33.2, which was Rubens' time. I was almost eight tenths faster. This was a real confirmation for me of all the work we'd put in. It gives you a real boost, because the emotions you have are so intense. These highs and lows you experience in a season make the sport so worthwhile.

'Any racing driver who thinks logically will usually try to drive at the limit. Anyone who goes beyond that is slower because you skid on the corners and ruin the tyres. You also risk spinning off. I have never said to myself, oh, there's a large run-off area at that corner, I can try it at full throttle and see what happens. At every corner, I try to find out where the limit is. I have a feel for it. But to find that limit, I do have to drive — albeit in a controlled fashion — faster into that corner than perhaps seems possible. This is the only way I can find out how far I can go and the only way to get to the limit and discover if it has not yet been reached. This limit I am talking about relates to the car because survival for me goes without saying. I am not in the least bit interested in ignoring the car's limitations and putting my life at risk. Never. I want to get to the point where what the car is capable of is being exploited to the full.'

This palpable pleasure in driving, the enthusiasm for every perfectly negotiated corner, this is what makes a *racer*. Frank Williams, head of the Williams team, once said that the difference in class between Michael Schumacher and other drivers could be explained by Michael's dedication to his sport. Ross Brawn, technical director at Ferrari, and a friend from the Benetton days, describes Michael as "without doubt the best driver I have had the privilege of working with. His strength for me lies in his bond with the team. His solidarity with them is absolutely essential, since it makes everyone in the team try automatically to give of their best. From a technical point of view, Michael is also always up to speed when we are at the development stage with a new car. He takes the trouble to keep himself informed, and that gives us extra motivation because he is so on the ball. And as for his driving ability, I can only say that Michael gets better and better. He can not only be very quick over one lap, he can also maintain that same rhythm consistently. He never eases up, and that sometimes allows me to employ risky strategies. The number of mistakes he makes is incredibly small, even when he is under extreme pressure.'

Team Ferrari: Inside the Legend

It certainly wasn't *amore a prima vista*, love at first sight, between Michael Schumacher and the Scuderia Ferrari. Rather the opposite. Even the contract negotiations in summer 1995 were awkward: what other driver would have kept Ferrari in suspense for so long? After all, the great Ayrton Senna had offered his services to the venerable Italian racing stable shortly before his tragic death. But Schumacher virtually had to have his arm twisted. The negotiations dragged on for a good twenty-four hours, first in the Hotel de Paris in Monaco, and then, when they had been politely ushered out of there, in Michael's apartment in Les Cyclades, Fontvieille. Jean Todt still remembers how suspicious the young man was, and that he 'meticulously copied every single piece of paper'. It was his manager Willi Weber who saw the potential in a Schumacher-Ferrari alliance, and convinced the 26-year-old to sign.

Today, Michael shakes his head in disbelief: 'At the time, I had no understanding of the magic of the name. I had no sense of what lay behind it. For me, it was just a team like any other, and because I had also had a very good offer from McLaren, I couldn't see the difference. I thought, they are both great teams, although in fact at the time McLaren seemed to be the more ambitious of the two. I'm so glad now I made the decision I did, it was the best thing that could have happened to me. I'm working with friends, achieving great things, and making lots of people very happy. Things couldn't be better. When, for example, you are standing on the winners' rostrum at Monza and you see the faces of the *tifosi*, then you can only feel overwhelmed by so much love and passion and admiration. For me the Ferrari myth are the *tifosi*. Their passion, the emotions they feel for this red car are boundless. I believe that once you have experienced this enthusiasm, it stays with you for ever.'

But back in 1995, the experience was still to come. Myths, dreams, legends, had always been alien concepts to the sober realist. He had always been a pragmatist, someone who lived in the present, thinking solely of his next step, as if that was the only way possible. Even as a child, he was never one to hang on the fence at race tracks and beg drivers for an autograph. He would often be asked later whether his Formula One career was the fulfilment of a childhood dream. His first response was invariably to raise eyebrows. 'I lived in Kerpen and the go-kart track was my world. Formula One was beyond my wildest dreams, I never bothered with it. Any old crate on wheels suited me. Formula One was completely remote and out of my reach, which is partly why I had no posters of the great drivers on my bedroom wall. I just wasn't the kind of child who had idols.'

As a boy in Kerpen-Manheim, he loved tinkering with go-karts. He could work up enthusiasm for the Dino Junior go-kart because that was the first kart for youngsters, and up till then he had driven grown ups' cars, but the luxury make Ferrari? 'For us at home, cars were the means to an end, no more than that. They were usually old, and when they were finished, we bought another old banger. It wasn't until later that I learned that a car could also be a luxury article, that aesthetics and style could be involved.' A lesson he would learn from the best teacher: La Ferrari.

'I have never been a dreamer. Even at the stage where I was working my way through the formula classifications, I always tended to be pessimistic. I was satisfied with what I had. Because Formula One was considerably more than I could ever have envisaged. I always thought, good, if the next step happens, wonderful, I'll have to grab the chance. But at the same time my attitude was always realistic. I never wanted to hope for things which might never become reality. I have always been a rather pessimistic person.

'During my Formula Three time, I recall watching a Formula One practice at Hockenheim. During pre-qualification I noticed the difficulties Bernd Schneider was having in a poor car, and he is a superb driver and was Formula Three champion at the time. I didn't feel that I was on the same level as him. That's why I never thought I might be able to drive a Formula One racing car to the proper standard. I thought to myself, *that's out of your league.*

'When the opportunity arose to test the sports car for Mercedes, I thought: *Oh my God. I'll never be able to achieve the times which the old pros did.* Only when I noticed that my lap times were good, even though I was driving well within my limit, did the penny drop: *Hold on, it might be much more simple than you think.* So, pessimism has usually brought me pleasure, usually because it leaves me happily surprised.

'Being a pessimist does not mean that I have more problems in difficult times, although up until now I have been spared real crises. It has been quite the opposite because in those moments I have always been sufficiently self-confident to get through them. After I broke my leg at Silverstone in the summer of 1999, I didn't know whether I would ever be able to drive as well again. I was pessimistic, and then once again was pleasantly surprised. And, at the climax to the 2000 season in Suzuka, I didn't always believe that I would pull off the World Championship. Häkkinen was two, three seconds faster in the first part of the race. I was battling it out behind him, trying everything, and said to myself, this can't be right. It sparked something off in me, I tried more and more new things, and somehow it worked. I have two very different reactions. If I see that things are not going as they are supposed to, it makes me fight and I am forced to address matters head-on and in positive terms.

'Having said that, after an accident, the next time I am in the car I don't drive all out straightaway. For example, after the serious accident on the Mugello test track which was caused by a technical defect I kept something in reserve for a while.

'Fate is a part of life. Whether in racing, or off the track. I've no problem with that. That's why broken suspensions, defective brakes, or a shattered underside are not so important to me. At first, I attributed the serious accident when I was testing in Monza mainly to a driving error on my part. When you come to this conclusion, you start to have your doubts. Why is the car getting away from you, why can't you get it back under control? If there's a technical explanation, it sets your mind at rest. You have the technical data, you know what can be done to ensure it doesn't happen again. And then you can live with it.'

Ferrari is the only team which has from the very beginning belonged to the elite club of teams which make up the Formula One World Championship. Looking back, it's hard to imagine that Michael is already the longest-serving driver in the history of the Italian racing stable. The 2003 season will be their eighth year together, longer than the entire career of most racing drivers. It began as a marriage of convenience — the twice World Champion in search of a challenge and the prestigious racing stable in search of success — but the union has long since become a highly regarded symbiosis. The initial friction has been smoothed away to produce a unity which has made perfection its watchword. 'I was once heavily criticised for saying, after visiting the factory for the first time, that Ferrari's engine workshop looked like my mate's at the go-kart track. However, Ferrari is now a team which is up-to-date in every respect. But I have never claimed that that was due to me. Without my team, I would be nothing. As I have always understood it, Formula One is a team sport.

Starting with the people in the factory at Maranello, everyone contributes to my being able to sit in a car like this.'

After a race, Michael never forgets to thank and to praise the team, and to stress that the team's the thing. Team principal Jean Todt respects this attitude: 'Michael never complains, even under the most difficult conditions. He always gets on with things, and never expresses the least criticism. Exemplary is the word for it. He has a leaping horse engraved on his heart, and the whole team, or rather everyone connected with Ferrari, has boundless admiration for him'.

This team spirit is due in large part to Todt himself and also to the milieu which the sovereign far-sightedness of Ferrari President Luca di Montezemolo has created for his drivers. Ferrari is above all an Italian make. In the old days it would have been unthinkable for foreigners to have any say in running it. Today — alongside Italians — a Frenchman, an Englishman, a South African and a Brazilian all have leading positions, woven together by Montezemolo, who recognised that la Scuderia had got bogged down in destructive in-house politics in the 1990s. Tradition, valued so highly by la Scuderia, was also holding it back. Todt lured Schumacher, Ross Brawn and the designer Rory Byrne to Maranello, leading to a situation unique in motor sport, where four old friends were working closely together, and with tremendous success. Schumacher, who is described by his manager as a 'harmony person', has incredibly high regard for this working relationship.

'Over the years, our relationship has become more and more harmonious, intensive, friendly and relaxed. Every year we get to know each other better, we share more and more experiences, which, thank God, have been overwhelmingly positive. We had a lot of negative and difficult moments, but we overcame them together, and this brings you even closer. People often asked me in 2002 whether too much harmony couldn't also be counter-productive. I don't think so. We get on so well, it makes it easier to work on the details. Everyone knows what everyone else means, and there is great transparency and trust within the group, so that there are no misunderstandings when we criticise each other — an advantage not to be underestimated.'

A dark-green Fiat Multipla is cutting corners on the narrow roads between Bologna and Maranello. The autostrada is jam-packed, which is why Michael has chosen this route. 'Does anyone know where we are?' he asks the people in the back, and laughs. Corinna is sitting in the front next to him. It is still quite hot, even though it is nearly nine o'clock in the evening. They are on their way from a function in Bologna and want to get to Maranello quickly, to the Ristorante Montana, and Rosella. But passing through a little village, Michael suddenly asks, 'Anyone want an ice cream?' and parks the Multipla directly in front of the entrance to an ice-cream parlour.

The two tables outside are occupied, a few men are standing at the counter and look up, somewhat disgruntled. The look says it all: Who's parked in that outrageous fashion? The man on the left of the table interrupts his conversation and looks up, but inside they've resumed chatting. In Italy they take a relaxed view of these things. Corinna pushes open the door, goes in, and orders five ice creams. At the table inside, a woman looks towards the counter, straightens up on her chair. The man outside also gets up and tries to see into the dark interior of the car. Corinna comes out of the ice-cream parlour, Michael opens the car door from inside, and at that moment its light goes on. The man outside and the woman inside both gasp — 'Shumaker?!' The other guests get up and run outside. But Michael backs up, then puts the car in forward gear. A laugh, a wave, then he drives off, leaving ten speechless people behind, who also start to laugh. They've missed their chance.

Scenes like this happen all the time when Michael is in Italy. At the toll barrier between the airport and Maranello, the weary man in the booth looks twice as he hands over the change — 'Shumaker?!', but the barrier is already on its way up and Michael is accelerating. The element of surprise is in Schumacher's favour.

Except in the 'Montana'. When he opens the wooden door to the restaurant and goes in, heads turn and jaws drop in astonishment, but Rosella is already at hand. Rosella is the landlady of the Montana, and she says she loves 'Mikele' like a second son. Effusively, but always with overwhelming sincerity, she goes up to the Ferrari driver and embraces him warmly. She takes his face in both hands and plants 'un bacio!', a welcoming kiss on each cheek. She then draws him into a little room on the left, at the back of the restaurant, which can be closed off with a sliding door and made private. Or she takes him straight down the steps, where, opposite the kitchen, there is a kind of living room for the family while they are working in the restaurant. It has a table with an embroidered table cloth, a sideboard with photos and various knick-knacks, a sofa, and a television which is never off. If he's with the team they'll eat in a private room, but this is where Michael sits when he's alone.

The Montana is quite simply a shrine, a chapel full of Ferrari kitsch. Shortly before the exit for Maranello, you come over the famous bridge where, during testing, the *tifosi* and the camera teams stand in order to get a clear view of the roaring Ferrari. But if, before the bridge, you turn right into a street which looks as if it's going nowhere, you will have reached your destination. On the first sharp right-hand corner is the *ristorante*, which has recently been extended and decorated. The architecture is a mixture of mountain hut and the functional, otherwise everything exudes 'La Ferrari'. On the walls in wooden frames are signed photographs of all the drivers, past and present — *'con grand amicizia', 'per la grande Rosella', 'grazie tante'*, from Alesi, Berger, Schumacher. A helmet from Luca Badoer, an overall from Eddie Irvine, old newspaper cuttings, the walls are one big collection of memorabilia. Little models of Ferraris, ashtrays with the prancing horse, flags, maps and in the middle of it all Rosella and Maurizio, her husband. When Michael can't manage to get there to eat, he at least pops in for a quick cappuccino, or just to say ciao to Rosella. She, for her part, brings him pasta every day for lunch at the track, when he is testing in Fiorano, the Ferrari circuit in Maranello.

'That's what I love so much about Ferrari: the warmth of the people connected to the team. This is not purely a working relationship, it's like coming to visit friends. All the people here are incredibly nice. That wasn't, of course, one of the things I took into consideration when I joined Ferrari. I didn't know about it at the time. But that is how it turned out, and today I feel very much at home here. I have learned as well that, among other things, a bit of improvisation is essential. I used to think that in this business it was a bit of a hindrance, but it can be really effective.'

In the long years of working together, both sides have probably found this middle way by subconsciously moving towards each other. Michael has loosened up a little, and the Italians have perhaps learned that striving for perfection can also be a virtue. And above all the Italians have learnt that not shouting about your feelings doesn't mean that you don't have any.

◆

At Monza on 10 September 2000 something happened to prove this. Michael was in the obligatory international press conference, in which he had always maintained careful control. Behind him were the blue FIA panels, and he was being quizzed about the important victory he had just achieved which kept open the battle for the World Championship. He was also asked whether this, his 41st win, which brought him level with Ayrton Senna, meant much to him. Michael, as so often, was staring straight ahead, his fingers toying with a bottle of water. But then, he seemed to clutch at the bottle, and uttered a hoarse 'Yes'. The journalists immediately in front of him, hardened professionals, suddenly looked up with fresh interest. Michael let out a painful sob. The rest of the journalists stared in astonishment, as Michael was seized by a fit of crying. He convulsed, trying to hold back the tears. For the first time he had lost his self-control in public. It was as if someone had ripped aside the protective visor with which he usually keeps his feelings hidden. With great effort, he brought the press conference to an end, and fled the room.

'That whole day was all too much for me. What had happened in the previous races: two retirements and two second places in races we expected to win. The fear that once again we wouldn't win the title. Knowing how vital it was to win here at Monza in a Grand Prix which means so much to me. Then the tremendous load off my mind. The enthusiasm I could feel on the podium. The thought of Ayrton whom I admired so much, and his death in 1994 — all this came back to me. The injury to the marshall — I didn't hear about his tragic death until later. And then on top of all that, that same afternoon one of my old friends suffered a heart attack. It was a strange mixture of things welling up inside, and somehow it all just had to come out.' On his way to the interviews with the television stations, Michael felt uncomfortable and wished the proverbial earth would swallow him up. He looked very vulnerable, very young, very helpless. Very likeable. No trace at all of the regal racer. There is no need for him to still feel ashamed, 'But I do' he answers quietly, looking down at the floor. The day after the win, *BILD* newspaper carried the euphoric headline: 'Schumi, we have seen your heart', and Italy's biggest sports paper *Gazzetta dello Sport* admitted with some amazement: 'Schumacher cries without shame and shatters the image of the ice-cold pilot we all knew.'

One year later at the press conference a few days after winning the World Championship for a fourth time, a journalist and Michael, both smile. 'You cried again,' said the journalist with a feigned note of reproach. 'Have you become a bit too Italian?'

Admittedly, it took a while for Italy and Michael to become close. It was difficult at the beginning and the situation was far from simple.

'They're bringing *him* in, of all people, to sort things out!' thought the Italians. The enemy, the man whose two triumphs with Benetton, the other Italian Formula One team, inflicted such humiliation on the unsuccessful Ferrari show team. This man is to be our salvation? The Italians were deeply sceptical. Hadn't they spent two long years trying to talk down the achievements of this German by attributing them to his calculated aggression? Did he have any idea just what he was being offered: tradition, myth, passion, cult of personality?

No, he didn't. This word 'myth' was foreign to him, it wasn't in his vocabulary. Nor was 'exuberance' or 'euphoria', qualities which the *tifosi* had loved so much in his predecessors Berger and Alesi. This Schumacher, by comparison, was so cold, so German. Totally goal-oriented, and without a shred of emotion. He wasn't even capable of *pretending* to be overwhelmed by the sense of history surrounding Ferrari or of at least feigning admiration for the myth, as others had done. No wonder he had received a somewhat frosty welcome in Italy. No sign, at the end of 1995, of that up-front affection enjoyed by other drivers solely for committing themselves to Ferrari. It was much more a case of suspicion — and mutual to boot. He was circumspect and mistrustful. They were touchy and jumped to conclusions.

Very soon an outcry of monumental proportions was echoing across the Alps. Germany had just got used to the successes of its new hero and showed less understanding than Schumacher of the fact that rebuilding takes time. 'Schumi, get out of your red cucumber,' urged the biggest-selling newspaper in picaresque fashion after the first failures, with a photomontage of a red cucumber on slicks. The *tifosi* were left gasping at this sacrilege.

That summer of 1996 saw the worst period in the Schumacher-Ferrari story. The reds were plagued by a series of breakdowns, and greeted with malicious gloating from all sides. External pressures mounted. 'If I have to name a difficult time with Ferrari, then that was it', Michael says. 'In the autumn, we were facing complete disaster, and I don't know what would have happened, had we not won in Spa.' Jean Todt would have been sacrificed, but Schumacher threw his support behind the man who had become a close friend in the months of hard grind together: 'If he has to go, then I go too.' The German and the Frenchman, kindred spirits in temperament, became extremely close in this difficult period — so close, in fact, that Jean Todt often speaks of his being a second son alongside his real son Nicolas.

'When you go through such hard times together, and see that the other person is not giving up either, and maintaining his enthusiasm for the work, then you develop a relationship such as the very special one — of which I am very proud — we have today,' says Michael.

In the end, there remained some hope of improvement after the botched beginning to the season. Technical director Ross Brawn and chief designer Rory Byrne, old friends and recognised specialists from Schumacher's Benetton days, had announced they would be joining Ferrari in 1997. Admittedly, they would not be able to work miracles straightaway — Formula One, the so-called king of motor sports, is much too difficult for that — but at least the spectre of hopelessness which had dogged 1996 had been banished.

Despite his Ferrari being inferior to the Williams, Schumacher managed to keep the battle for the World Championship the following year, 1997, open until the last race. But Michael's act of desperation in that race in Jerez threatened to damage a relationship with Ferrari which had, even in the eyes of the Italian public, become more settled. Having rammed his Ferrari into Jacques Villeneuve he compounded the disaster by refusing to admit that the mistake had been his. In many interviews since he has acknowledged his error, but the incident, and his initial reaction to it, once again clouded his relations with the Italian press.

'If there is anything in my career I could undo,' he said much later, 'it would be that episode'. The word 'mistake', which all the reporters wanted to squeeze out of him at the time, he now uses freely when talking about the affair. But at the time, the press, particularly in Italy, were churning out the old story that the illustrious racing stable had embarked upon a kind of *mésalliance* with this Rambo of the race track. 1998 saw the development of a non-aggression pact between Schumacher and the press because despite having hopelessly inferior tyres in the first part of the season, Michael had once again managed to keep the title decider on a knife edge until the last race of the season. Would it finally happen this time? Would Ferrari win its first Drivers' Championship since 1979?

On the second start at the Japanese Grand Prix, Michael stalled due to gear-box failure, and had to make the second restart from the back of the grid. He drove the fastest lap, but Mika Hakkinen in the McLaren-Mercedes was crowned World Champion. And then when he was celebrating the win with Mika Hakkinen in the Karaoke bar — just as Hakkinen would do with him in 2000 — the Italian press all howled: 'And we thought he only drank milk!'

With the new year came new hope. Ferrari President Luca di Montezemolo once again expressed his hope to the international press that this would be the year of a Ferrari renaissance. It had to be. And the season began well, delivering an exciting personal duel between Michael and Mika. Then came the race at Silverstone on 11 July, 1999. Schumacher's rear brakes locked coming into Stowe, at a moment when the race had already been stopped. Because his radio was faulty, Michael didn't yet know this, only that he was in pain. 'When I put my foot down hard on the brake pedal, I knew straightaway it was going to be bad. And to be honest, there are much nicer feelings than heading full speed, and without brakes, into a pile of tyres. There are also nicer experiences than getting badly hurt. I've been lucky, it has only happened once in my career.'

Michael hit the tyre wall at 107kph, breaking his right leg. 'Silverstone was one of the worst moments of my career, if not the worst. I remember it very clearly because it was so strange. After the impact I tried immediately to get out of the car. It was instinctive to try to get out but I was stuck. I couldn't get my legs out of the cockpit because the tyre had been forced through the chassis and that's what broke my leg. It was terrifying, trying to get out and not succeeding. Finally we managed and the doctors told me to lie down on the ground. And then what happened was so weird, I really thought I was going to die. I was lying on the ground, and all around me everything went dark and at the same time I heard my heartbeat getting louder and louder, but slower and slower. It was something you read about or see in a movie. As my heartbeat got slower, everything got darker, and suddenly my heartbeat stopped. I couldn´t hear anything anymore. It probably only lasted a couple of seconds, then the sound and light returned but I do remember that everything was so intensely still.... In that moment I thought: that´s it.

'I had had several accidents before, some of them serious, but until Silverstone nothing had happened to me. But as soon as I knew what had caused the accident, had analysed and could explain it, I was able to cope with it.' And there was no escaping that it was the end of his World Championship hopes.

There was a further unusual development for Michael because he suddenly had to cope with the fact that his team mate Eddie Irvine was now in a position to win the coveted Drivers' Championship for Ferrari for the first time in 21 years. 'I was very torn over this. It would have been hard for me to see Eddie taking the trophy which I so wanted the team to have. On the other hand, like everybody else, I was a part of that team and, like them, I wanted to achieve the goal we had been chasing for so long.'

Stronger than ever, Michael returned for the last two races of the season, to lend Irvine all the support he could. But in the climax to the 1999 season in Suzuka, Irvine began to feel the pressure, was too slow, and found himself 45 seconds behind Michael. But Schumacher was unable to make any impression on the powerful McLaren-Mercedes. Hakkinen was once again World Champion.

It was only at the beginning of the next season, on the evening of 9 February 2000 that Michael felt that he had a car which was equal to those of his rivals. A car that would have excellent prospects in the battle for the next World Championship trophy and with which the suffering might be over. After winning the 2000 title, Jean Todt, who had suffered as much as anyone, reflected: 'I can recall exactly Michael driving over the line in first place, and all the emotions of the mechanics, the flags waving. I had an immediate feeling of perfection. We had finally achieved what we had been working for all those weeks, months, years. I waited for Michael in the enclosure and embraced him. I thanked him and, before climbing on to the podium for the official victory ceremony, said to him that our professional relationship would never be the same again. I said that, regardless of what might happen, things had changed for ever. Which turned out to be the case.'

The door up there on the left of the garage is still locked, and has been for quite a while. The blinds on the little window are closed tight. No chance of a glimpse inside. A small white piece of paper on the yellow painted door says 'Scuderia Ferrari Marlboro', making it clear that there is no entry for unauthorised personnel. It is late Sunday afternoon in Suzuka, on 13 October 2002. The last race of the season finished some hours ago and the World Championship has been decided since the summer. A few stairs below, in the paddock, Norbert Haug and Mario Illien of McLaren-Mercedes, a few journalists and the physiotherapist Balbir Singh are waiting for that door finally to open. Balbir looks at his watch, shaking his head in disbelief. There's still nothing happening. Someone fetches a round of beers. Mario Theisen from BMW-Williams joins the group and has a beer pressed into his hand. The season is over and it's time to celebrate before everyone goes their separate ways and starts working towards the 2003 season. Ralf Schumacher strolls past, looks up at the locked door, and grins knowingly. He joins the others and has a beer. Then the door opens, and a Ferrari engineer steps out. He looks down, sees everybody relaxing in the paddock and rolls his eyes, half amused, half irritated. He speaks briefly into his mobile, then goes back inside. The group below starts to laugh. Scuderia Ferrari Marlboro: they have won everything, and yet they're still hard at it.

The team briefing after the obligatory press conferences at the end of the final Grand Prix of the season in Japan in 2002 lasted over an hour. Ferrari had once again achieved a double victory, the ninth of the season, with Michael Schumacher the undisputed winner. The day before Michael had ordered twelve bottles of white Bacardi ('not the brown, the white is better for mixing, and we'll need a lot of Cola too'), dead certain that he would be able to celebrate at track side with his friends, colleagues and fellow competitors. He had achieved everything there was to achieve: his fifth World Championship, winning it after only 11 out of the 17 races, making him the fastest to the title in the history of the sport, with more victories in a season than any driver before. Despite all this, he was once again buzzing with ideas and suggestions which he was bursting to get off his chest before the winter break commenced. Something has struck him during the race: hadn't he already asked for an additional function on one of the 19 buttons on his steering wheel? This ought to be fitted now, it would certainly give a small extra advantage. He was so absorbed in his own world that he didn't notice how the time had passed and that all the engineers around him, all world champions in their field who would soon have to start grafting hard on the new car, would have liked to simply get on and celebrate.

The door opened again and men dressed in red swarmed out of the briefing room. Everyone down below looked up expectantly: two, five, eight men appeared, but Michael was not among them. He was still locked in discussion with his race engineer Chris Dyer. They were the only ones left in the bare room, amidst all the laptops. Outside it was pitch dark. Four bottles of Bacardi had already disappeared from the fridge in which Balbir had stashed them. Someone had discovered the hiding place. Haug, Illien, Theisen and Ralf had also disappeared. In the paddock, they were tanking up in preparation for the traditional karaoke night. When Michael finally joined them after another half hour had elapsed, Balbir had to dash off to fetch fresh supplies from the fridge.

This scene epitomises Michael's approach to his profession. Never letting up, giving meticulous attention to every detail, getting to the bottom of every problem, and always looking for new solutions. Sepp Herberger, the legendary coach of the winning German football team who won the 1954 World Cup once said, 'After the game, the game is only beginning.' Michael, an enthusiastic part-time football player, shares this view and he has also taken to heart another piece of football wisdom, the title of a book by the journalist, football reporter, director and cabaret artist Sammy Drechsel, 'If you want to win, all eleven of you must be friends.'

At around ten o'clock Michael left the little room to go back to his hotel, to get changed for a late supper and the karaoke night. Back in the Ferrari garage, the mechanics were still scurrying around, everything bathed in glistening bright light. The cars had been dismantled and packed in large crates ready for loading into the Jumbo jets and the return flight to Europe. The crates had been swathed in red tarpaulin and tied with thick rope for safety. The team were tired, their red trousers completely filthy, and they were looking forward to finishing and going for dinner at the hotel. But then a moment's carelessness from one of the team who walked into the path of a forklift truck loaded up with one of the huge crates and as a result his right ankle was broken. As always before he left the track, Michael looked in on the garage to say goodbye. The injured mechanic was lying on the floor, with all the team members gathered around him, not knowing quite what to do. Michael was immediately transformed from partygoer into the logical racing driver who has to make quick decisions and issue precise instructions. He sent someone to fetch Sid Watkins, the Formula One doctor who was just about to leave the track. Someone else was told to go to the Race Office and organise emergency transport. Short, sharp questions: 'Which is the nearest hospital?' 'Where is the interpreter who speaks Italian and Japanese?' Somebody had to find him, and bring him back to the garage. When Watkins and his colleague arrived, they put the leg in splints. The ambulance arrived and Michael bundled the interpreter into the back of the vehicle, giving him his mobile number with instructions to ring immediately with the most important information: which hospital they had gone to, how was the mechanic, who was the person to speak to. After they finally drove off, Michael at last left the track. By then it was the middle of the night and too late for dinner. When Michael arrived at the restaurant, straight from the track and still wearing the same grey T-shirt, the meal had been cleared away. So the World Champion moved straight on to the karaoke hut.

Test day in Fiorano, Ferrari's private track in Maranello. It is late August, and a very hot Saturday afternoon. It is already Michael's fourth test day working from 9am to 7pm, and therefore, for the mechanics, from 7am to 10pm at least. There is not a breath of wind, backs are soaked with sweat, faces in the garage glowing with the heat, but the driver will simply not ease up. Out of nowhere a small delivery van drives up to the garage, and a man in dark red livery gets out and takes a folding table from the vehicle. He sets it up, spreads a yellow table cloth over it, and puts out canisters of ice cream. In the meantime, a second man has lent a ladder against a tree and fastened an old bell to it. The ice-cream man has arrived, secretly organised by Michael. Admittedly he had wanted a real ice-cream cart, one with a bell, but even in Italy this is hard to find at the drop of a hat on a Saturday afternoon. But not for nothing is improvisation one of the great Italian arts, and so it is that the mechanics are lined up like schoolboys in front of the ice-cream man, with the driver in their midst. Everyone is laughing, prodding each other — great idea, typical Schumacher.

It is just such spontaneous ideas as these, the little gestures, which typify Michael's leadership style. He is always observing and evaluating what he sees. If everybody is wiping the sweat from their foreheads, if their movements are becoming involuntarily sluggish, then a break is needed. A spell of relaxation will help them to once more give of their best. Much of this happens unconsciously. Michael never allows himself a weakness in front of the team and as a result they themselves unconsciously make that little extra effort. Because he always gives one hundred per cent, every one of them also seeks to do the same.

When Michael leaves the garage, you can feel a slight slackening of the tension and when he enters it is possible to detect a tightening of the mechanics' concentration. It is the natural authority he radiates, the respect he commands, and of course his successes, which bring about this virtually imperceptible difference. It is also the fact that he would never let himself go and inflict his bad mood on them, he would never pass the fault for a bad result down the line, or attribute blame for a poor performance to the car. He would never raise his voice unreasonably, should something fail to function properly. 'In my view it is important to give people support, to make them stronger, particularly when they have made a mistake.' He wouldn't describe his way of working as a leadership style: 'It is no good shouting and pointing the finger of blame, it is much more important for someone who has made a mistake to recognise it, and above all to know where they have gone wrong. It's nothing to worry about, we all make mistakes. We are all human. It is vital, however, that we do not make the same mistake twice. And I find that works. Reproaches don't, they are not acceptable. I have never been one to raise my voice. Yelling is not my style. I am pretty even-tempered, at home, as well as at work. Shouting and screaming, as far as I am concerned, never do any good.'

What *is* needed is staying power, concentration, focus. The ability to immerse himself completely and intensely over long, concentrated periods is what distinguishes Michael from most people, and is one of the factors which separates him from other racing drivers. Talent, character, natural gifts, not mental training, as many have supposed.

'That's the way I have always been. If something interests me, I give it my total, undivided attention and devote myself to it to the exclusion of everything else. Someone might speak to me, and I wouldn't even hear them. My wife Corinna could tell a tale or two about this. Sometimes I'll be reading the paper and she'll say something to me, but I am so absorbed I won't hear her. At the beginning, when we were first getting to know each other, it was sometimes a problem. But Corinna soon realised that I wasn't doing it on purpose, and now we see the same thing in our daughter. She's just like me. When she's taken up with something, she cuts herself off completely.'

And then there is his adaptability, the capacity to adjust in a flash to changed situations in an 'appropriate manner', as they call it in Formula One. Although this has been developed through years of practice, it is innate and also not consciously schooled. According to Ross Brawn, Schumacher is, more than any of his colleagues, able to drive at the limit, but at the same time to digest what is going on around him. This allows him to rethink or change strategies during the race.

'He can fulfil his role as Formula One driver, and has additional free capacity to think about the race and what is happening all about him,' Brawn says. 'Sometimes I get him on the radio, and it's as if you and I were talking now — you would think he was sitting next to you and doing nothing. In contrast, I have worked with drivers who just about manage to cope with what they are doing at that moment, but have nothing spare. That is the difference between him and normal mortals.' Schumacher himself regards this as probably his greatest strength. In addition, he also seems to have a mechanism in his head which enables him, when problems arise, to sort out what is important from what is not. To pick and choose, that is the secret. It enables him to avoid the insignificant and let his thoughts leap rapidly ahead. 'Everyone is like that in motor sport. We are all so taken with the goal we have set ourselves that we are constantly preoccupied with it. Sometimes it's a bit strange, since we have scarcely achieved the goal before we start thinking ahead, and are barely able to enjoy it. You just lose valuable time thinking about missed chances, there is always a next stage that you want to reach.'

Occasionally it seems as if the victories are being ticked off in businesslike fashion. After a race some will be celebrating, and others will already be packing away the cups, tables and chairs. It is, however, merely a consequence of the rapid world in which he works. 'When you are part of the work process, you are speedily brought back to reality. You savour the success for a very brief moment. Sometimes that is a real pity, but it is the rhythm we are stuck in. When I am alone, and something reminds me of a particularly sweet moment, I can still enjoy the success.'

Race-Day: A Grand Prix in detail

The changes in regulations in 2003 bought some canges to the race day routine, but the one thing that never changes in Formula One is the early starts. In fact, one of the first things to learn about Formula One is that it means getting up early. The race courses are usually not situated in the immediate vicinity of the hotel, so the journey takes some time, and the first briefings take place very early. For Michael it is important that the hotel is close to the course, and not whether it has a jacuzzi. In Barcelona, for instance, a lot of the drivers stay in the city because it is very beautiful and has correspondingly fabulous hotels. Michael usually stays close to the motorway exit in an unspectacular single-storey building which could hardly be described as very beautiful, with tiny, stuffy rooms and dark brown walls. But the journey to the track takes barely ten minutes, an irrefutable argument when it takes other drivers a good 45 minutes to get from Barcelona itself. Michael's luxury is the extra minutes he can spend sleeping.

Formula One is often underestimated as a sport. Not least because the faces of the protagonists are not visible through their helmets, making it difficult to convey the struggle, tension and strain they have to cope with. And so, as common prejudice has it, the driving is done by the car.

'Some people consider that my profession involves driving around in circles for a bit. And on those weekends when there is a race, a bit more driving around in circles. A bit more often than usual, twice a day, and three days in a row, one after the other. And that's about it.

'I could easily dismiss these remarks as the prejudices of cynics, opponents of motor sport and ignoramuses, but this is more or less how most people imagine my job. At any rate, I am often asked what I get up to on a race weekend, after the practice laps, the qualifying laps and before the actual race. The question is often delivered in a latently reproachful tone in which there is a slight echo of envy about my do-nothing existence. And I have to admit, you don't get to see much of me on a race weekend. Probably not nearly enough for my fans, nor for my taste. But there is a quite simple reason for this. As is the case with test driving, a weekend such as this doesn't just consist of driving, but of many other obligations. The word that encompasses these obligations, the word that on occasion drives to sheer desperation those who want to, or have to get in contact with me is: briefing. And 'Michael is at a briefing' is probably the response which friends, relatives, mechanics, journalists and guests of Ferrari most frequently get to hear.

'The first briefing is on Thursday at 14.30. It is always held at exactly this time because by then everyone has arrived, and half an hour later the major FIA international press conference takes place which is the traditional and official curtain raiser to race weekend. All of the drivers, Jean Todt, Ross Brawn, and the boss of the Ferrari press office, take part, and we chat briefly about the latest bits of news and about matters to which possible consideration must be given in conversations or interviews. And because I am quite often booked in to do that press conference and there's a fine for being late, I'm always having to dash to the interview room where around 400 journalists and the other drivers are gathered. After that I have to face questions from television channels from all round the world in the specially separated off 'pen', down in the paddock. Only then can I finally get down to what's most important: popping into the pits and saying hello to the engineers and mechanics. Then I normally drive round the track, which is one of my jobs as president of the drivers' association, the GPDA.

'Safety has always been extremely important to me, and since that terrible weekend in 1994 when Ayrton Senna and Roland Ratzenberger died, it has been even more so. We point out which parts of the track could be improved, and then one of us must check that we approve of the changes. Then there are nearly always one or two exclusive television interviews, sometimes photo-shoots, or other brief appointments before the first technical briefing of the weekend begins at 17.00 with Jean Todt or Ross Brawn, and with engineers, and the engine, tyre and aerodynamics people. This is when we chew over things from the last race, and make suggestions for the upcoming one.

'On Friday we get down to the real matters in hand. My usual timetable begins with a 9.30 am briefing when we discuss various suggestions and tactics for the practice session. There are often camera teams waiting for me when I leave the truck, and I try to give a few brief interviews. Then from 11.00 to 12.00 there's the first practice session, and this of course is followed by discussion of any small modifications to be made or suggestions for improvements. I have a quick snack before the second practice session between 13.00 and 14.00. More TV interviews follow, and lunch. Another briefing at 15.00. This is often a lengthy business because my first impressions have to be compared with the initial telemetric data. Everyone is completely concentrated and gives a brief report on their particular responsibility, be it tyres, engine, gearbox, suspension, aerodynamics etc. We might, for instance, discuss particular gear settings, or the shock absorbers, or the overall impression of the car's performance.

'Then, at around 16.30, I usually have to give one or two longer TV interviews, and at 17.00 there is a drivers' briefing organised by the FIA, at which I am accompanied by our team manager Stefani Domenicali. At 17.30, back at Ferrari, there's another briefing at which there are the first concrete proposals for the car's tuning on Saturday. The engineers and specialists have now evaluated all the data from the practice sessions, and are in a position to make specific suggestions. These will be discussed even more carefully at the next briefing at 18.30, but then that's it for the day, at least as far as briefings are concerned.

'Saturday is always the hardest day, purely from the point of view of time. The first briefing at the track starts in the morning at 8.00, which means having to get up really early. The technicians report on their final, overnight modifications, and we also discuss the weather report. I don't usually manage to have any breakfast beforehand, and take my muesli and tea into the meeting. From 9.00 until 9.45, and then 10.15 until 11.00, there is another practice session, and in between there is barely any time for proper discussions.

'At 11.15 there is another briefing, with the mood even more serious and concentrated. Times are compared for the individual lap stages, the various opinions are collated with a view to deciding which set-up, which tyres, what settings for the springs, wings and so forth should be made for the qualifying laps. These can be tough decisions, and are sometimes made on the basis of gut reaction. Almost always this briefing merges seamlessly into the next at 12.00. Then, it's a case of preparing yourself mentally for the qualifying laps between 13.00 and 14.00.

'Sometimes I manage to snatch 20 minutes sleep beforehand, which does me good. If I am among the top three, I have to go directly to the international press conferences — two for television, one for the press — and then at 15.00 there's another briefing. All the data and impressions of the car's performance in qualifying are analysed and reviewed. This debriefing takes place with the whole team, and then with a select group, including Ross and the race engineers.

'If I have missed the press conference, there is usually another opportunity for the German and Italian print and radio journalists to grill me about my drive. Only then do I have a chance to take a breather and switch off, or sit and relax and chat with Corinna and friends. But not for too long, because the evening is yet again devoted to briefings.

'This is the point at which, slowly but surely, we finalise plans and tactics for the race. So, a briefing at 18.00, briefing at 19.00, and then supper. I love the Spaghetti Aglio è olio which our cook makes, and often devour a gigantic portion of it. When, at around 21.30, I finally leave the track, I am invariably dog-tired, and just want to go to bed. It is great that Balbir is always around to give me a good massage which helps me sleep.

'Sunday, and the tension mounts. The first briefing is at 8.30, and we talk about last minute modifications and things learnt from the previous day. Warm-up is from 9.30 to 10.00, and immediately afterwards we get together for a briefing, and any last-minute thoughts. After that I make my way to the Paddock Club to have a few words with the guests of Ferrari and the sponsors, shake hands, answer questions and sign autographs. There is not much time now, since the drivers' parade is at 11.15 and we are driven round the circuit to give the spectators the chance to see us without our helmets on ... for us this is virtually the only opportunity to get an impression of the spectators, since later, in the car, you can neither see nor hear all that much. Except at the very end, if everything has gone smoothly.

'At 12.00 there is the final race briefing where we once again discuss strategy. And then I usually try to switch off until 13.30 when the race gets underway. I look for a spot where I can sit quietly and, above all, stretch out. In order to relax, I have to lie down. Sometimes I have to make do with a large box, as in Brazil, where the pits are relatively small and the drivers have limited space because the motor homes are not there. I will just lie down on a crate, close my eyes, get my breathing rate down, and go to sleep, just for a short time. Oh, and then, one last briefing. After the race, after the press conferences (hopefully), and before the celebrations (hopefully), at 16.30: the debriefing.'

The timetable is a tight, constricting straitjacket for the drivers. There is little time for idle chitchat. No wonder that many observers complain that the drivers are remote prima donnas. This is the impression which can spring to mind when you see the boys in their overalls dashing through the paddock, looking neither right nor left. 'This is what I often have to do,' Michael admits. 'I am usually so preoccupied with something, or with the topic which we have just talked over in the briefing, that if I were to loosen up at that moment and make eye contact, I would lose track and get distracted. And, back at the briefing, it would take longer to get back on the ball. Or, I know that I have an appointment to keep, and have very little time, so I try not to get held up.'

This is his celebrated focus, the so-called tunnel vision. From Thursday to Sunday his field of vision narrows perceptibly, as does his readiness to discuss abstruse topics. Then on Sunday, the procedures are so well-honed, that any change is disruptive. And the only real ritual which the world champion needs before the race is his nap.

'I always take one. The length varies and it depends how long the last briefing lasts. Sometimes, I just drop off for a short while, but I can also sleep soundly for half an hour. I have been doing it since 1998. I don't remember how it came about, but since then I've always made a point of finding time for it. It is simply more agreeable if I manage to rest, though whether I actually need it, I don't really know. But it's nice if I can stretch out for half an hour, an hour, it does me good. Even before a decisive race, I never feel so worked up that I can't sleep. That has nothing to do with it. There are some nights before a race when I don't sleep so well. But then I reckon it's less to do with what's going on in my head than for example with the change in time zones.

'Sometimes, I go through phases during which I simply can't sleep. I often wake up in the night, or am unable to drop off. I don't think it's the stress related to the race which disrupts my sleep. It is more often stress related to other things which I have to do as part of the job. Meeting the press, for example, is a big pressure and, as for everyone, there are often also private matters which I have to attend to.'

Rituals consist of regular events, and they, in their turn, have to do with security. This is of course also true for the people around Michael. For his wife Corinna, for instance, who admits: 'When I'm not at a race, I always go upstairs to my room at 13.10 to be on my own. I know that Michael is ready then. And at 13.15 exactly I ring him on his mobile. I always call to wish him luck, and it drives me crazy if I can't get hold of him. But this hardly ever happens, and if it does, he calls back. He knows that I have tried to speak to him.'

And then? It is hard to imagine what goes on in the heads of racing drivers moments before the start. Michael himself finds it very difficult to explain. 'How tense you are, how agitated or relaxed, depends on so many things. It varies with your mood, and is different for each and every person.' The sequence of events, however, is always the same: 'First, you go on to the grid. I talk to my race engineer to make sure everything is fine with the car. Then there are often interviews before we do another check to see that everything has been set up as discussed. After my final visit to the lavatory I get into the car and make minor last-minute adjustments to my seat.

'Then comes the intense concentration and I have about two minutes to collect my thoughts. Sometimes I make a conscious attempt to clear my head of everything, only when it's overwhelmed. It depends what has happened during the build-up. Sometimes everything is hectic and stressful because something's not right with the car, and it has to be sorted out. Then, of course, I get worried. But sometimes I am completely self-confident and totally relaxed. On occasion it's been the case that I was just about to become World Champion, and I knew that everything was fine. But I was still worried on those occasions. Somehow it's always different. That's what makes it all so exciting. Once the engine has started, it's essential to concentrate on the car and just exclude everything else before the start.'

The woman at his side. That's how she is usually described. Or the strong woman in the background. His support, his mainstay. When describing Corinna Schumacher, the reporters love reaching for clichés. That's what happens when you shut yourself off from the public so consistently and that's what happens when you are married to Michael Schumacher, a man who every second Sunday puts his life at risk.

That's not the way Corinna sees it. Or rather, that's how she seldom sees it. She knows Michael, she knows his passion. She trusts him. For her, Formula One is just as much routine as it is for him, and racing Sundays are as much a part of her life as they are of his.

By the time Corinna opens her eyes on a race day morning, the man next to her is already awake. He grins and plants a kiss on her forehead. He has to hurry, a Sunday raceday starts early. Michael has a quick shower while Balbir, his physiotherapist, waits outside in the car which is ready to take them to the track. Michael pulls on a T-shirt, rubs a little gel into his hair, dries his hands on a damp, white towel and after giving Corinna a quick kiss, he grabs his briefcase, and is off. The towel is left lying on the floor. Corinna gets up, leisurely. She has time to take a long shower.

'Sometimes, when I look at him, I get a tremendously deep feeling of happiness. I look at him, and think: that's my husband. It's a marvellous feeling. Michael is so strong, and so tender, so full of energy, and so profound. He is a good man, and a completely devoted father. The four of us make a great team.'

A driver picks Corinna up from the hotel. She too has had nothing for breakfast, and will make up for it in the peace and quiet of the motor home at the track. She has all the time in the world. That early in the morning there aren't many other people in the paddock, and the meetings Michael and the other drivers have leave hardly any time for private matters. Briefing, warm-up, another briefing, Paddock Club, drivers' parade, briefing — the drivers usually don't even manage a visit to the motor home. Time is always short in Formula One. Balbir prepares some fruit muesli for Corinna from the mixture he makes up for Michael.

'The wonderful thing is that nothing is too much for him. Never mind what, when, or where — it's always OK. I have never heard him groan, roll his eyes, or say: later, no more now. Michael is a doer. He simply gets on with it, as if nothing creates difficulties for him. That is a great feeling, it gives you a sense of security to know that when he takes something in hand, it will get done. He'll manage it. Everything will soon be sorted out. I love that. And somehow, you can go to him with anything, ask him anything. If there are certain things I am unsure about, I just talk them through with him: what do you think about this or that? And somehow, he always has an answer. Somehow, he always gives the impression that he has things under control.

'But the best thing is that we always discuss things thoroughly together, and he never retreats into the role of being (supposedly) the stronger one of us. Instead he absolutely insists on listening to my opinion and then he accepts it. That is one of Michael's basic characteristics: he accepts that in many areas other people know much more than he does, and then he seeks out their opinion. He is interested in loads of things, particularly when he has never had much to do with something before and therefore knows next to nothing about it. He often comes and asks my advice, a kind of tit-for-tat in our relationship. Somehow, each supports the other in whatever's going. Sometimes, when things get too much for me, or I get really up-in-arms about something, then he exerts an unbelievably calming effect. He will say: just stay calm, I'll do it. He is simply not the sort to hesitate. He has usually got an answer for everything.'

By this time Corinna is in the motor home, killing time. She has met a few friends, and they are sitting at the table chatting. Corinna often has photographs of horses with her, and she loves to talk shop about riding or breeding. In Formula One she often meets people who are also involved in her favourite sport, such as Patrizia, for instance, Nick Heidfeld's girlfriend who is an enthusiastic and talented Wild-West rider. Finally, after midday, Michael comes back. He sits down with the women for a cappuccino. These are the first ten minutes that he and Corinna have been able to spend together this Sunday race day.

'When we first got to know each other, right at the beginning, Michael was always playing jokes. This got on my nerves at first, because he was always coming up with some new prank. If I was sitting down somewhere, and suddenly got a glass of lukewarm water tipped down the back of neck, I could be sure it was him. I know that he doesn't often give that impression from the outside, but the man can be incredibly funny. Michael likes to laugh with other people, and about other people. This is one of the things that I really love about him. We sometimes laugh ourselves silly about something trivial, something completely insignificant. We simply have a lot of fun together. You know that from the moment you fall in love with someone it's often the case that even the smallest things can be funny. To be honest, it's the same now as it was in the beginning. I think that's amazing, considering we have known each other half our lives. We can still chat for hours on end. When there's a weekend free, we often get in the bath together in the evening, and talk about what each of us has done that day.

'With Michael, everything is so harmonious. It feels as if there is a link between us, at all times. We are always touching each other, we do it automatically. We simply have to. Our children now do it, too. When we are eating, for example, we all sit very close together. Sometimes, I have to laugh, because we are pressed up so closely together that we can hardly eat. And it's not as if we don't have a large table.'

Michael and Corinna can't really expect to be left undisturbed in the motor home. Photographers and cameramen are jostling round the door, hoping to capture that intimate moment. There are, of course, other guests sitting around in the motor home — friends of members of the team or guests of Ferrari, and everyone wants 'just a quick photo' with the world champion, or an autograph. No chance of a quiet conversation. And so, retreat. Michael takes Corinna by the hand, they go to the bus, and up the steps into his little room. Just a few more minutes together, then Corinna leaves. Michael is asleep. This is the only ritual which is important to the five-times World Champion. A period of deep relaxation before the extreme exertion. His physiotherapist Balbir wakes him up, gives him a massage, gets him ready for the race. Corinna is sitting down below; her thoughts are with him. She plays with her fingers, rings, necklace. When Balbir comes down, she rushes off once more to Michael, before he goes to the pits. A long kiss, and then he is off.

'Michael is such a family man. One of the reasons why I love him is the way he is with our children. He always has time for them and it is wonderful to see how much he enjoys it. He is never happier than when playing around with Gina and Mick. He is always thinking of things to do with them, climbing, trampolining, playing around — those sort of things rather than singing or reading with them. That's where I come in, Michael is the more active one. He can hardly ever sit still. We never spend the day sitting on the sofa together, or simply hanging around. Never. He is incapable of it. Obviously, we sometimes watch a film together, but afterwards we get on with things again. He is unstoppable. He's always has to be doing things, and he always finds something. He has a go at everything. And, above all, he can do everything.'

Before the race starts, Corinna tries to find somewhere to sit where she can't be seen by the cameras. In the office of Ferrari's race director Jean Todt, for instance, sometimes alone, sometimes with friends. She always keeps her fingers crossed, and often has both fists clenched in front of her mouth. Blow three times on both thumbs, for good luck. Now, she too is tense. Until the race is underway. Then she relaxes, but her fingers stay crossed for the whole race.

'I am not really afraid for Michael. I know a lot of people find that hard to understand and that they say, "How can she stand it, knowing that her husband is going off, and may perhaps never come back?" That's not the way I see it. Perhaps, if I am totally honest, I suppress it. But that's the only way

I have ever known Michael, as a racing driver. I have absolute faith in him, in his strength, his judgement, his temperament. Michael will always be a dogged fighter, battling to the end, but he is not a gambler. He never takes unnecessary risks. He is much too sensible for that. He knows when there's no longer any point in taking someone on, he simply waits and mounts an attack later. Knowing that that's the way things are, helps me of course. But, to be honest, there are days when thinking about the race gives me an uneasy feeling — along the lines of: what if I can't explain it, it's just part of the routine. Sometimes I worry about it, sometimes I don't. Since Michael is not out there on the track on his own, my anxiety comes mainly from what the other drivers might do, from situations Michael might get into which are beyond his control. Don't misunderstand me. In general, I think all Formula One drivers are good drivers. To get where they are, they all have to know what they are doing.'

Corinna remains silent and withdrawn throughout the race. The wife of the world champion knows all about her husband's sport. For both of them this is their natural environment. She knows what a racing driver has to do to stay in front, or to get in front. They often talk about it, because Corinna wants to know everything about what he does. So, as she watches the race, she follows it expertly and just occasionally, at critical moments, she has a sharp intake of breath and blows three times on her thumbs.

'Another thing which really fascinates me about him: when something's new to him, he takes a long, hard look, gets to grips with it, and he can do it. If at first he is not quite sure about something, he looks for a while — and when he tries it, somehow it clicks. Take skiing, for instance. I was better at it, because unlike him I had done it as a child. And what happens? After a year, he's whizzing past me. It was the same thing with riding. He gets on a horse, and can do it. He sits there and looks as if the only thing he has ever done for years is ride. Anyone else would take two years to get to that point. It drives me crazy! I train hard, make a real effort, and he does it just like that.

'Well, of course he can't do everything. Painting, for instance, would not be up his street, no matter how hard he tried. But he certainly has the talent to study things very exactly and make them his own. Enviable. On the other hand he also takes a lot of trouble with other people. At go-karting, for example, he loves nothing more than sorting out someone else's kart, getting it in top shape, giving people tips. He can't get enough of it, and he loves it when he sees I am having fun. He could never have a completely unsporty wife, or one of those doll-like creatures whose only concern is to look immaculate.'

It depends, of course, on how the race is developing, but it usually doesn't take long for Corinna to relax. Ultimately, she can see what is going to happen. Her fingers are no longer knotted together.

'Michael is unbelievably honest. This was one of the things that struck me about him after we got to know each other, when we were 16 or 17. There were a few occasions, playing cards for instance, when I really noticed it. Cheating? Out of the question. Michael never would; is somehow incapable of it. Something in him would always resist it. Which is why I have never understood those stories which came up at the beginning, about Schummi the cheat, and so on. I got more worked up about those stories than Michael did. It was a complete mystery to me how people could believe them. Then I noticed that all those people didn't know him as I did. This will probably never change, and somehow it doesn't seem all that bad. Nevertheless, I still get annoyed about it, and think: I beg your pardon? He is the most honest person there is!'

If a race has been particularly important, Corinna will run over to the pits just before the finish. She wants to stand at the front by the barrier so that Michael can see her when he gets out of the car. The cameras are there, but she just ignores them. The main thing is that Michael knows she is there. This is important to him and to her. A long kiss, then he has to leave. The presentation ceremony, press conferences, eating with the team... it isn't until the evening that Michael will be free again, and then, together, they will fly back home, and to the children.

Testing and Training

The morning of the test drive is cool. It is fresh and bright over Mugello, the mountain range between Bologna and Florence where Ferrari's second race track lies. It is a spectacularly beautiful region, hilly but forbidding, not as friendly as large stretches of Tuscany. Down in Scarperia, the people say there are wolves in the mountains. The mechanics in the garage are exhaling small clouds of air, working concertedly on the red structure which they will soon have transformed into a professional racing machine. The interior of a Formula One pit is reminiscent of the intensive-care ward of a hospital: everything scrupulously clean, mysterious tubes feeding into the stomach of this shape which lies propped up, naked and without its red skin, illuminated by brilliant white spotlights. Men in red uniforms — they could be doctors' coats — beavering away at this corpus, poking measuring instruments into pipes and meticulously recording the results, shining their pocket torches on to connecting bits, constantly gathering to examine and study the data flowing from ubiquitous laptops whose screens are alive with strange lines and squiggles. They agree that everything's fine, the patient is thriving and is ready to become a racing car. The mechanics begin to assemble the machine.

Just before 8.30, a dark-blue Maserati draws up next to the Ferrari motor home. Michael, wearing blue jeans and a brown leather jacket, tips the driver's seat forward and collects his black bag from the car. He steps into the motor home, and goes straight to the driver's cabin. Behind it is the cramped space where he stays during his test drives, gets changed, and has a massage. He pulls on his overall. The briefing begins at 8.30. In the meanwhile, his physiotherapist is preparing his simple breakfast of a balanced muesli mixture and herb tea. He takes this to the other motor home where he sits with the engineers and discusses the test programme for the day. Shortly after 9.00, there is the characteristic roar of a Formula One engine from the garage, full-throated at first, almost threatening. At full revs, it is painful to the ears. The engine is being warmed up. The door to the briefing truck opens, the first engineers step out and go over to the garage. Michael comes down the stairs and takes the few steps to the garage, with a typically energetic spring to his stride. The test day can begin.

The garage which houses the car spare parts, tyres, wings and engines, fuel, oils, and grease is separated by red partitions from the telemetric area. Everyone who works here is a specialist in his field. The engineers sit in front of their computers and can track every movement of the car, connected by hundreds of sensors to the telemetric system. As Michael comes into the pit to greet his 'guys', as he calls his team, his racing engineer comes up and tells him that the car is ready. Outside in the corridor there's a small table which, like everything here, is painted red, where Michael's helmet, the gloves, and ear plugs are kept. Over the course of the day there will always be a bottle of electrolyte drink, Michael's mobile, or the letters which have been delivered to the race-track office left on the table. Michael puts the plugs in his ears, carefully draws the fireproof hood over his head, followed by the helmet, and the gloves. Then he goes over to the car and climbs into the cockpit from the left-hand side.

In a modern Formula One car, the driver's position is closer to lying down than it is to sitting, and the bucket seats are made to measure, so it is no easy matter to get into the seat. Finally, he swings both elbows down and in, and the mechanics bend over and fasten the seat belt. A quick wriggle, to make sure everything is snug, and then Michael raises his left hand to signal that the engine can be started.

It is just after nine o'clock when the red car drives slowly out of the garage, disturbing the tranquillity of Mugello. Michael does just a single lap, the installation lap, then he comes back to the pits and clambers out of the car. All the systems now undergo a check to make sure they are working properly, leaving Michael time for a pot of tea.

The treadmill test then begins. Michael takes the car out for a few laps, then returns to allow minor modifications to the car. Out again for a few laps more, if possible under the same conditions so that the results are properly comparable, then in again. A touch more wing, out again, in, no the wing position was better before. Let's try it with another setting for the suspension, back in, back out, in between getting out of the car, discussions with the engineers: is the time difference a result of the different adjustments or the different tarmac temperature? Surely it's got warmer outside? Does the amount of time gained justify that amount of rebuilding? How does this particular blend of tyre compare with the previous one?

This is attention to detail at the highest level. 'It's sometimes exhausting,' says Michael. 'Sometimes you spend three days going round and round, and don't make an ounce of progress. That is frustrating for all concerned. But then, if we suddenly take a giant leap forward, a new idea, a concept, something which makes the car a second faster, then we're on a high, and all that grind seems worth it.' Every time the car is returned to the garage, the specialists descend on it like the photographers do on Michael whenever, anywhere in the world, he enters a racing circuit. The tyres specialist measures the temperature of the tyres and the depth of the grooves. The brakes specialist assesses the temperature of the brake discs. Everything from the engine, cooling system, tarmac and external temperature are constantly being monitored. In the garage, no one raises their voice, the atmosphere is one of work, and of high concentration.

This is the other side of Formula One, and one which is rarely seen. It has nothing to do with models and money, high heels and helicopters, or VIPs and police escorts. Television seldom penetrates this far. It is the side which reeks of petrol and not of perfume. Of paint, not catwalk. For the drivers, this is the real world of Formula One. And it is not remotely glamorous.

Midday, and an hour's break. The mechanics and engineers stroll over to the motor home, and the awning beneath which a lavish Italian buffet has been assembled. Michael is sitting at the table, and is already eating. A salad, then pasta, fish or a lean steak. His break is constantly interrupted by interviews, photo opportunities, a statement on behalf of a sponsor, hand shakes, and always an unending stream of German and Italian TV reporters in need of soundbites for the evening news. There is never enough time, and he usually doesn't even manage to get in a brief massage before the test drives get underway again. The same rhythm follows in the afternoon — a few laps, a report on his impressions of the car, a few pointers, discussions, off again, back to the pits, constantly at the ready. The boss of Ferrari motors, Paolo Martinelli, says of the most successful driver in the rich history of his racing stable: 'He can describe the behaviour of the engine at every point of the track. He knows what his priorities are, and doesn't ask for everything at once. And if the car isn't to his liking, he still knows how to get the best out of it because he knows how to adapt his way of doing things.'

One of Michael's strengths is his ability to operate at the same level throughout the whole day. This makes reading technical data considerably more reliable, since the probability that lap-time differences can be attributable to variations in Michael's performance is negligible.

'He can drive very consistently, every lap to within a tenth of a second, which is invaluable. He can describe precisely the feel of the car, and he knows what he wants,' says Rory Byrne, Ferrari's head of aerodynamics. 'He is really a tremendous help for every engineer, because he enjoys test driving and has an eye for those crucial details which can make all the difference. And he also has this ability to get 100 per cent out of the car in only a few laps, and to evaluate it precisely. That's ideal for an engineer, particularly when you are developing a new car because it's extremely important to understand the weak points of the old car in order to move forward. I know immediately what my new car can do. Michael is very good at this, he can help us to pinpoint exactly those areas which have to be improved. And he is a constant source of new ideas about how this can be done. He loves all the technical aspects, and wants to understand everything.'

Despite so many years of experience of motor sport at the highest level, Michael never succumbs to the temptation to approach similar, recurring problems with the same solutions. This goes against his firm conviction, that it is always possible to do a little bit extra. 'Problems are never quite the same. Even if the diagnosis is the same, the car has changed from one race to the next, and even more so from one year to the next. The same diagnosis suggests something different. The problems in Formula One are therefore always new, always different. There are never model solutions to getting a secure grip on things. After a while experience does help us to recognise the problem quicker, but how we then solve it varies.

'There are, of course, certain basic procedures which you can follow. If the car is understeering, you can experiment with a bit more front wing for instance. Nevertheless, the conditions or the problems are always different, and we are always having to probe, and test and tinker. This is what I find so interesting, otherwise things would get boring.'

As a trained car mechanic, Michael knows about cars, and he feels very much at home in the workshop atmosphere of a Formula One garage. 'I love sitting in the garage and watching the guys work on the car — I try anyway to keep an eye on my car as much as possible. Though these days I usually don't have much time.'

During testing Michael never gives the impression of being bored, uninterested, or irritable. He always seems motivated. He wouldn't even be able to tell you what attracts him most about his profession: driving the car or tinkering with it, racing or testing. 'It's difficult to say, because everything is so different. I can get just as enthusiastic, and be just as happy, when I drive a great test lap, if I have the feeling that everything has gone to plan, as when I do lap after lap at racing speed on a test drive. And then, in the race itself there are moments when I am involved in quite emotional duels, where I have to battle it out and assert myself. And if it comes off, then I am on a high. Or in qualifying, if I get everything right and the lap goes well and the time is spot-on, that's great.

'But what is very special, is change and the development of the car, our strategies and my driving over time. It is inevitable that there will be moments when nothing goes right and when we don't seem to move forward. For instance, we might have a Friday practice when we can't get the tyres right. I start worrying, I drive and drive, and things aren't working out. We just can't get things sorted. But then when we do turn things round on Saturday, it gives us another high. All these different, rapidly changing emotions over the course of a weekend. And then, when it finally all comes together — and, thank God, it frequently does — that, of course, is an even greater experience.'

weeks the trainer rang me up, and asked me if I could come over to the track. I got there just as they were starting their run, and very soon Michael was well ahead of Stollenwerk.'

Schumacher was so committed to training, and over-ambitious, that he once strained his knee, and for some time had to carry a niggling injury. Thanks to the professional attention he now receives, this would never happen today. He follows a balanced fitness regime, designed to improve coordination and stamina. His results are phenomenal: on a test day in Mugello in summer 2002 an ECG measurement gave him a top pulse rate of 151. After coming off the track and achieving speeds of 220kmph, it was just 140.

Sheer strength is not so important for a driver, with the exception of the neck muscles. Michael exercises his neck muscles with a special apparatus which he sits in, like a cockpit, with a helmet attached. Then he bends his head to the right, then the left, while at the same time lifting weights. 'The transverse acceleration during a race, or the deceleration forces when braking, are extreme in Formula One. The lateral g-forces are four to five times your body weight, and they last for almost the two-hour period that the race lasts. On top of this is the added weight of the helmet, another 1.5 kilos. This strain is usually just on one side, since most tracks are right-handed. So I have to do special training for Brazil, as this is a left-handed track. I remember in Formula Three, before I ever drove a race car, I once drove in Dijon, and after ten laps I could barely hold my head up straight. As I was driving, my head had just tipped to one side, even though I had come up through the ranks and had some racing experience.'

And so he punishes himself, with that consistency so typical of the man. He trains several hours a day, and even in the evenings after a test day. When everybody else is hanging out exhausted in the motor home, he is in the mobile fitness centre, pedalling away, lifting weights, doing his stretching, for two hours in the evening. When he is not testing, his regime involves a day of training, four, six, even eight hours, depending on what stage he is at in his training programme. During the build-up for the season he puts in the longest sessions.

'Out of season I train on average five or six times a week, mainly stamina work on the bike. Then in the power room I do some neck exercises, chest and loin muscles, which are designed for my particular needs and to stabilise the spine. My fitness advisors make sure I put no strain on the joints and work with low weights and lots of repetitions. I mostly use free weights, and not machines. I also play as much football as I can, which is enjoyable and never boring. Variety is important. That's why I have taken up climbing which is also good for strength and stamina. It's a good mixture. You have to avoid the bike training becoming tedious, which is why I have started to cycle outdoors. Two and half hours on a cycling machine can get you down.'

During the season, especially after long flights, it is sensible to shorten the sessions. Rest and regeneration are a very important part of any professional sportsman's regime. According to Dr Peil, 'Michael's recovery rates are sensational. He is more consistent in his training than anyone I know. He punishes himself, then punishes himself a bit more. He gets the maximum out of his talent. And the individual attention he gets protects him from the overload which is often the undoing of top sportsmen.'

Public Property

Red helmet, red car. After all, red is for passion, red is for love. He is common property, and for more than a decade he has been a welcome guest, visiting us in our living rooms every two weeks of the season with predictable regularity. We know him. Little children shout 'Schumi' enthusiastically when the little red man once more hops in the air. And fathers clench their fists. When he wins, they win a little with him.

Does this mean they own him? Is a public figure obliged to open his or her heart? Can someone well-known be unknown? Does someone who can drive a car better than anyone else in the world also have to be able to speak, describe, express his feelings well? Is he allowed to reveal only what he wants to reveal?

Famous actors love playing roles, even in public, but Michael finds this difficult. Every public appearance requires him to overcome his natural disposition. He is very reserved and does not like to be the centre of attention. But he also doesn't like any insecurity to show. This sometimes caused him problems, especially in the early days when he would try to disguise his discomfort with a kind of abrasive casualness. It made him appear aggressive, pigheaded and unfriendly. Instead of the calm and serious individual which he naturally is. Nowadays Michael is older, more experienced and successful, and much more at one with himself. His inner calm is transparent and his earnestness more considered. He has acquired a sovereign air, as an elder statesman of the sport.

There is no doubt that his success has helped, not just in being accepted, but also in bolstering his confidence. The feeling that he has paid his dues probably plays a part in this. He grew up with the feeling that he owed many people. There has always been someone who helped him, who supported him in this expensive sport, and to whom he felt particularly indebted. A patron, a benefactor, a financial backer. People, for example, like Gerhard Noack who out of enthusiasm for Michael's abilities put a go-kart and his tuning expertise at his disposal. Or Jürgen Dilk, the father of a boy his own age who first lent him his son's kart, and then later — year upon year — would take the young Michael with him to the races. Without him, says Michael, he would never have made it to Formula One, because Dilk, at a decisive moment, stood security for him. Or Adolf Neubert, who allowed the teenager to practise his tuning skills. Or Willi Bergmeister, who gave him days off during his apprenticeship as a mechanic because he could see how important racing was to him. Then Eugen Pfisterer and Helmut Daab who enabled the young Schumacher to get his first Formula King drive. According to Michael, this was 'an absolutely great time' for him, his fellow driver Joachim Koscielniack, and the mechanic Peter Sieber. Or Gustav Hoecker who provided him with the car. And then Willi Weber, Michael's manager who first gave him the money for his expensive Formula Three drive and later secured him a start in Formula One. Or his father, who gave his son whatever support he could, and sometimes went beyond his means.

Michael still dutifully answers every question put to him by the media, though when he is asked the same one for the umpteenth time, he has been known to show his irritation. These are the moments when he comes across as something of a know-it-all. 'I find the game with the media rather difficult. A half-hour press conference is more strenuous for me than a whole race. It's just not my world. I am no actor, and everyone tries to put a spin on everything about me. I'm also not someone who can account for his feelings at the touch of a button or even want to. When I have crossed the line over an hour before, and am on my tenth interview, my sense of pleasure has understandably diminished.'

Michael and the international media have worked and interacted for many years now. On the one side are the journalists with their 'stories', and on the other is the man who is always at the heart of those stories. Schumacher, the most powerful driver of them all, someone who is master of ceremonies, artistic director and manager rolled into one, is also simultaneously the main player in that theatre which every two weeks of the season stages the drama of Formula One. It's a one-and-a-half-hour long advertising spot, subsidised by all the world's biggest brands. This son of a man rents who out go-karts in Kerpen has for years been the starting point and focus of the media interest which fills the coffers of this particular theatre: exposure determines market value, market value determines exposure. It is not surprising that the journalists try to glimpse behind the mask, and that he tries to make it even more impenetrable, and to preserve his private life. With some success, but not entirely to the satisfaction of everyone.

'I have to admit that it's very difficult to really get to know me. It takes time. I find it very difficult to open up straightaway. I can only do that when I know the people. I find it hard to behave as if someone is my best friend when he certainly isn't. My general attitude is one of healthy scepticism and this has been strengthened by certain events in my life. Formula One has shaped me in this respect. The dilemma is that there is just one of me, and on the other side there are hundreds of journalists who have to write and report about me. They can't all get to know me, especially because on the weekend of a race I have other things to do and am therefore barely available.'

It's no wonder that this leads to misinterpretation and misunderstandings. Difficulties often arise because in this global sport people from diverse nations and cultures communicate in languages which are not their mother tongue. And there have been hurtful things, too. Michael finds it hard to understand when he is criticised for an impeccable performance, simply because it appeared to have been too smooth or unspectacular. And it hurts when he has frequently been accused of being a machine, a robot, or a computer. He is a sensitive man, recognised within the Ferrari team as someone who notices other people's problems. Often he has been known to shut the door, turn to the person concerned, and ask them what is wrong. And he is the kind of person for whom the adoration he sometimes receives from his fans is embarrassing, such that on occasion he reacts to it awkwardly. On one occasion a small boy started crying when Michael had given him a much yearned-for autograph. The World Champion was so shaken that he quickly ruffled the boy's hair, turned on his heels and disappeared back into the motor home where he secretly wiped a few tears from his eyes.

'It's appalling how people keep on reading Michael wrong,' says his manager Willi Weber. 'He has, learned how to defend himself in this high-pressure society of Formula One, but he still remains a sensitive young man who attaches importance to the judgements of other people. Basically, he has remained the lad from Kerpen.' And Jean Todt, the Ferrari team boss, offers the opinion that 'Michael was let loose in this jungle at a very young age, and has learned how to defend himself. His supposed arrogance is merely a self-defence mechanism.'

Michael has very definite ideas about what he wants to reveal, and what he doesn't and rejects the assumption that a public person is also public property. As a racing driver he presents himself to lenses and microphones and answers questions about all aspects of motor sport as a part of his job. As a human being it is impossible to keep some things secret, and other issues he can talk about without revealing very much about himself. But as a father, it gets difficult. Family life is sacred, and in his eyes he has the right to maintain that privacy, even if it happens to be of great interest precisely because it is kept hidden. Normally, Michael regards enquiries about this area of his life as being intrusive, and persistent questioning will generally be rebuffed.

He is always direct, and at times can be brusque. And he never fights shy of conflict. Any discord has to be resolved immediately, with no beating about the bush. Since unresolved grievances can quickly lead to problems, he believes in talking things over as uncompromisingly as he would tackle chicanes on the race-track. He has of course learned how to cope with his status and with the fact that he is always under scrutiny. He has now come to terms with this, it has become routine, even though at heart he still doesn't really understand it. He would probably now describe his relationship with the media and public as 'reasonable' which is one of his favourite words and this is interesting when you remember that he drives fragile cars at crazy speeds for a living. And of course, he realises the fact that he has for some time been regarded differently, even if he is firmly convinced that he has remained faithful to himself.

'Hero status makes me uncomfortable. I don't want it, I have a problem with it, just as I do with the hysteria surrounding my person. Obviously I appreciate what people think of my achievements and how it lifts them but I don't see myself as a hero.

'*I am just like everyone else, I just happen to be able to drive fast.*

'I can't and won't play this role which has been concocted for me. I like watching football, get excited like everyone else when FC Cologne are playing, cheer when they score a goal. But that wouldn't make me go to the stadium to collect autographs. That is not important to me, never has been, even as a child. Fanaticism is alien to me. Which is why, I don't find it easy to slip into the frame of mind of many of my fans. I haven't really changed very much. When I was younger I always tried to keep myself under control, to keep myself hidden. When you are young you don't yet have the standing and the experience. That's why you try to avoid certain issues because people are always trying to read things into your responses, usually some weakness. You just don't know how to cope with certain situations. And then you try to hide your feelings, even when you don't really need to. The example which springs to mind is Mika Häkkinen and the comments which were made about his bursting out in tears in Monza. In my opinion there was a lot of nonsense talked about this. After a while, with time and experience, you develop a lot more self-confidence and a couldn't-care-less attitude which says "that's the way I am, write whatever you want". I think that this has something to do with maturity and age.'

It has not exactly been a smooth learning process. One of the most frequent reproaches directed at Michael was that he is incapable of admitting his mistakes. This makes him feel he has been treated unjustly. In fact he readily admits his mistakes and would do so openly and freely except that he is required to do it repeatedly and under pressure. Then the same spiral is set in motion and he feels he is being forced to feel a particular way about certain events. At which point he goes into his shell and rejects these demands, partly out of defiance and pride. Even to this day he is reluctant to accept that he is expected to play a role he has not chosen for himself.

Michael discussed this problem of public perception and pressure in an interview with *Stern* magazine at the start of 2001.

In response to being asked whether he agreed with Niki Lauda's characterisation of him as 'an emotional type, who was slowly becoming more charismatic and was beginning to build a car round himself.' Schumacher replied, 'I find it difficult to believe that since my success I am someone different. Sure, I am developing, but I am still the same person I used to be. You can't be charismatic from the very beginning. Gerhard Berger once described me as egotistical, without really knowing me. Today he sees things differently. As one of the next generation of drivers, you are in competition with the established ones, which is why they tend to stress your bad sides. It is nice that many of them are slowly coming to see me differently, but it's a pity it has taken so long.

'I feel more experienced than I used to. And I feel that people accept me much more. They don't try so often to twist something I say. Even if they do, I'm less bothered by it. In any case, there's nothing I can do to change it. Perhaps that's how I've changed. For a long time, I saw things as either black or white. I wanted to put right anything that had been misinterpreted. But I realised that doesn't always work. You just have to let certain things go. Perhaps I'm better at expressing myself now. When I was asked a trick question, I used to beat about the bush.

'However I balk at the idea that people only understand that I am a human being like any other when they get some kind of proof, such as me showing my emotions or making mistakes.

'Outside the public gaze you can see that I am a perfectly normal chap who from time to time has a drink with his mates. So far I have made few mistakes but do I still have to make a few more for people to see that I'm a human being? I just don't understand that. I am very controlled, because I am very well-balanced. It has to be something really extreme to make me lose control. And I don't think I have ever been as outraged as at Spa in 1998, over the Coulthard incident.'

When asked about his protectiveness over his family's privacy, Michael responded simply, 'Otherwise my wife and our children would often be recognised and couldn't move around so freely. That's the main reason. Incidentally, in the past, I often noticed that the wives of Becker, Stich, and many others were praised in the beginning for their openness, and then later were criticised for it. It was difficult then when something cropped up which they didn't like and they protested that it was none of the press's business. My wife and I decided we did not want to let this happen to us.'

Although there have been a few clandestine photos taken of Schumacher. 'The paparazzi don't always leave us alone. In the past, when we were on the boat in Monaco, they would take pictures. At home in Switzerland, and in Norway where we have a holiday home, they respect our privacy. If I were to live in Italy, however, no chance. We once had a holiday in Sardinia which was a complete wash-out. Paparazzi the whole time. If you know that, you don't go there any more. I have an eye for it. I look out for it, it disturbs me, and then when I know it's going on, I shut up shop. Everyone has to decide for themselves how they are going to cope. For us, it was clear from the start: Corinna would give no interviews because she doesn't feel comfortable doing it. Everyone now accepts that. And VIP events are not our world, it's all too superficial. I would rather spend my time at home with family and friends.'

When Michael's career is over, asks Stern, does he intend to dedicate himself to his family? 'Certainly, for a while I will be living only for them. But I must admit that since I've been with Ferrari — and certainly since our children were born — my priorities have radically changed. I cannot complain. Ferrari sees to it that I get enough distance from racing. Because they see it does me good, and that I derive my high level of performance from it. When I give up, I'll do it without knowing what I shall be doing next. That's the way I imagine it. I wouldn't want to jump straightaway from one thing into the next.'

Family Man

The little blond boy is fidgeting about on his chair. Being four years old and sitting still is not an easy combination. 'Can't I eat something now?' Mick grabs his fork, but his father restrains him.

'Just wait a minute, Gina and mama won't be long.'

But Mick is incapable of staying in the same spot for more than a minute. He slips down under the large, wooden table and reappears between Michael's trouser legs making a face.

Michael has to laugh. 'Come here, you're hot, let's take your pullover off.' Helping him off with his woollen pullover, Michael runs his hand over his son's tousled hair, and then plonks him back on his chair. A car drives up outside. Michael gets up and brings the food to the table. They're having schnitzel with rice and vegetables.

Gina storms into the kitchen with a drawing in her hand. 'Look papa, that's what we painted today' and climbs excitedly on to Michael's lap. Proudly, she waves the sheet of paper under Michael's nose. He tries to hold her arm still so that he can have a look at the picture. Corinna comes in more slowly, taking off her coat. She has collected their daughter from nursery school and now they can eat.Lunch at the Schumachers in winter 2002. One day of many Formula One free days.

'Gina, eat a little more quickly. Mick, would you like something to drink?' Normal everyday life. Mick doesn't like vegetables, and Gina thinks the gravy is too spicy. The Schumacher's house is just being renovated — 'It was high time; we have been living here quite a while' — which is why the family spends a lot of time in the dining room which exudes a reassuring cosiness.

Through a door and past two budgerigars there is a conservatory which the children have long since taken over. Mick drags his father there after lunch. He wants to be Spiderman, as he was when they went to the fair, and Papa has to help him search in the big box for the costume. The man for whom nothing is fast enough in his job, is sitting serenely on the floor rummaging through a wooden box with his son. They have found the trousers, but where is the top?

Gina shoots round the corner. She has a thick anorak on, and red cheeks. Quick, everyone outside! Mick is almost out of the door when Michael grabs him. 'First put your jacket on, you'll be too cold without one.' Corinna is outside, in thick jacket and boots, and is beaming. A friend has dropped by with the children's Shetland ponies and a little carriage which they can pull. Gina is delighted and runs up to the ponies while Mick follows in her wake. The dog Bonnie gives a startled bark. The other dogs appear from round the corner, and begin sniffing at the ponies. Michael disappears back into the house and fetches a camera. While Mick is clambering around on the benches, and Gina waits expectantly on the carriage box, the proud father takes a few snaps for the family album.

'I love days like this. They are moments in which I feel that the world has slowed down. I can really relax. In the evening I often play football, and all in all I have the feeling that we are a family like any other. It is very important for Corinna and me that our children grow up as normally as possible. We would like them to develop into people who recognise and adopt certain values and standards. That's why they haven't been brought up by nannies but for the most part by us and their grandparents. Both Corinna and I come from ordinary backgrounds and so we don't know anything different. We both think we had a great childhood, and we want our children to have one too. Obviously we can afford a lot more than our parents could, but then you mustn't want everything on a momentary whim, or out of boredom. That's what we want to convey to our kids, and we think so far we have managed it.'

The two sides to Michael Schumacher are very evident in his home life. One is Schumacher the racing driver: energetic, concentrated, focused on the essentials, goal-oriented. Always ready to go, always a step ahead. The other is the private man: softer, slower, more relaxed and patient. Even the sharpness of his features which seem so pronounced when he is inwardly tense seem to melt away. Along with his work ethic. At home it's fine if something doesn't get sorted out immediately. If it doesn't get done today, then he'll just do it tomorrow. In the job, that would be absolutely unthinkable.

If Michael is asked to describe himself, one phrase always crops up: well-balanced. If Michael is asked to describe his life, he says that he is perfectly contented. Despite the fact that he is an international star he finds his greatest happiness in the simple things of life — a rare thing, of which he is well aware — and he enjoys them to the full. 'I have a wonderful wife, we have two great kids and we are all healthy, I have been able to make my hobby my profession and I am successful. I am able to work with friends — what more could I want? That's why I try and enjoy it now.' He adds, with a grin: 'It won't always be like this with my work. I'm well aware that it can't go on for ever.'

He is a realist. A man with both feet planted firmly on the ground and he is kept there by a woman whom he has loved since his youth. After winning the 2000 World Championship observers had been amazed at how unflappable he was throughout the weekend and he was asked what part Corinna had played in helping him remain so incredibly calm. Michael said that her part was invaluable. 'It is not by accident that this weekend has gone so smoothly. I simply feel a whole lot better when my wife is with me. It gives me so much security. It's a great thing to have the support of such a friend and partner. The saying goes that behind every strong man there's a strong woman, and this is 100 per cent the case for me. She is an exceptional woman, and I am very grateful to have found her.'

How much strength Michael draws from his harmonious family life is demonstrated by another declaration of affection which he made on the same day. He was asked if he was looking forward to telling his children about his World Championship win. 'The feelings I have here today I share with the team and the tifosi, but my children are too little to really understand what has happened here. And I am pleased about that because they are what, on good days and bad, keep my feet on the ground. When I get home, I shall simply be a happy man who is coming home to see his children.' The private Michael Schumacher is, above all else, a man of harmony.

The family is his retreat. The force field from which he draws his energy. He would probably prefer to separate the private and the public person completely but he knows that this is wishful thinking. On the large, solid wooden table lies the previous day's newspaper. It has an effusive report about the house they have recently bought, complete with details and photos taken from a specially chartered helicopter, and with the banner headline, *Schumi's New Dream Villa*. Today the paper is frightening its readers with the lavishly illustrated story of the haunted house Schumi has purchased. The previous tenant, it seems, had disappeared under mysterious circumstances and the neighbours have heard noises. Michael gives the paper a derisive grin: 'Strange, how quickly our house has been transformed from a dream villa into a haunted castle. A good thing that Gina and Mick can't read yet, otherwise we would have a real problem. Only yesterday we were in the house and because I hadn't seen the cellar, we all went down and pretended we were cave explorers. It was really exciting for the children but I don't think they would have found it so funny if they had read that the house is apparently haunted. I don't think we could have even persuaded them to move in.'

Keeping the family out of Michael's public life as a racing driver was one of the main reasons for moving to Switzerland. The Swiss are unimpressed by so-called celebrities, particularly in the French-speaking region, where Corinna and Michael have lived for years. The family are left completely in peace. No paparazzi, no phone calls. Just a polite 'Grüezi' (good morning) when they happen to meet you taking the dog for a walk. Michael still talks about the time when he was walking the dog and met a woman doing the same. They spoke about the weather, how much it had rained, the dogs. The kinds of things you talk about if you live in the same village, but don't know each other. Not a word about Formula One. The woman didn't know him, she was just being polite. They said goodbye, and off they went.

There's not a single story about the Schumacher's home life in the press, and nor will there be. He will also never bring his children into the paddock because he doesn't want them to think that this 'artificial world', as he calls it, is normality. 'We also don't want them to think they are something special. That would inevitably happen if everyone ran up and photographed them. Of course they know that I am a racing driver, but they have no idea what that means. We want to keep it that way for as long as possible.'

Michael always has things clear in his mind: he looks as well balanced as his Ferrari in a good race. The Schumachers keep open house, and often have people staying. Corinna's parents, friends from Kerpen or elsewhere. Particularly in winter in Norway, most weeks are packed with activities and visitors. Ferrari's team principal Jean Todt comes for New Year's Eve or birthdays, along with brother Ralf or his former colleague Jos Verstappen. The tradition is for the men to go off on a mountain hut tour with snow shoes, sledges, and ski-bobs, overnight in simple huts. 'We cook and eat together, and then play cards or just talk. It is absolutely wonderful, there is such a deep feeling of camaraderie.' It's always the same: the simple things in life are the best. Even more so when they are a kind of luxury because they are so rare. Michael has photos, showing them all wrapped up and with red noses, their arms round each others' shoulders and looking challengingly into the camera.

Michael has had to learn to be calm. Initially it was unthinkable for the non-stop Schumacher. Stay still? Let calm descend? Isn't that a waste of time? That was how he thought, until forced to take a break. The accident at Silverstone in July 1999 was more than a sporting caesura. The heel was slow to mend, and Michael was compelled to be idle — at least, that's how he saw it. 'Corinna wasn't used to me not being able to keep busy. I felt I was a real burden. But she managed it well.' Three months later when Michael returned to the track for the last races of the season, and to help out Eddie Irvine in his battle with Mika Häkkinen for the World Championship, he was incredibly fresh. And drove more effectively than ever.

'I surprised myself. It wasn't as if I had felt worn-out before. Not at all. I always thought, better to do everything yourself and not take a break. But the fact was that all at once I found everything easier, I could feel that the break had done me good. It was as if my batteries had been completely recharged. I had real power and since then I try to switch off over the winter. I make no appointments, never test drive before January unless absolutely necessary. I don't go to galas or other functions, and reduce my training for a while. I try to take each day as it comes. A lot of people don't understand why I never go to prize-givings. I find that very stressful. There is always a great crowd of people, and I don't as a rule feel at ease on such occasions. During the winter I have to begin my training in order to maintain my rhythm. Then, when the season starts up again with the first tests and sponsors' events, my batteries are recharged, I feel fresh and really looking forward to things. I'm sometimes so well rested that I can hardly wait to get back in the car. And to my mind that's exactly how you should feel, particularly when you have been doing this as long as I have. A Formula One season is so long and draining, you simply have to be fit when it starts, physically and mentally fit.'

For years his credo seemed to be the more work, the better, but this has changed with age and experience. What other top sportsman, in any sport, has been in virtually uninterrupted contention for the World Championship title for near enough ten years? During this time, Michael has had to live with being the centre of public attention at every race, and having his each and every move minutely analysed. Switching off and hiding from the attention is a method of self-protection.

It is so hot here that the tarmac is boiling, and the heat is multiplied by the high-rise blocks. The concrete walls reflect the rays of the sun and a stroll through the city saps every ounce of energy. Michael and his friend have ordered a coffee on ice cream at a café, and are sitting outside on a stone bench. Elbows on their knees, they are happily slurping their ice cream-cooled coffee, and relaxedly watching the passers-by. Strolling round the city was pretty strenuous. A woman passes with her small child who is hot and bothered. The man with a guitar seems to be doing good business even though very few take time to stop and listen. But Michael and his friend do have time, they are here on holiday. Both have pulled their stetsons down over their faces. On account of the sun, not the people. Why should they? Not a camera in sight. What usually happens when Michael is in public is that someone will circle back trying to be unobtrusive, strolling along as if rather bored. But not here, there are just people in jeans and T-shirts who quite clearly don't give a damn. Next to them is a couple, the woman has taken off her shoes, and put her feet on the man's legs. She smiles across at them, somewhat embarrassed — the heat! Michael curses that he has put on jeans. And, at the same time, he is enjoying simply being able to sit here.

Michael enjoys telling how he was once able to sit drinking iced coffee in a public place. Not a single head turned as he walked down the street in Dallas, Texas. No driver beeped his horn, no-one pulled out their mobile, no animated whispering. No one recognised him. Not even in the evening when he had to show his passport to get into a club. The name Michael Schumacher produced no reaction. 'I'm normally always being watched. It doesn't matter where I am, or what I'm doing, people are watching me. How I eat, how I drink, how I am dressed — it seems as if everything is of interest. That's why it's so nice to be on the other side. Not to be watched for a change, but to watch.' His enthusiasm is understandable if you put yourself in his shoes. Then you realise how unusual this experience must be for him.

When Michael is asked about his dreams, his secret wishes, he responds quickly, and always with the same word: anonymity. He would like to be invisible, to be unobserved. There are people who enjoy being looked at. Michael Schumacher is not one of them. Even after more than ten years in the public eye, after more than ten years of regularly having camera lenses pointed at him, you can sense him tense up a little before facing them.

At the start of the 2001 season Michael was due to give a speech at the presentation of the new car at Maranello, the Ferrari headquarters near Modena in Italy. All Michael had to do was to say a few words, but he wanted to speak in Italian, so he had specially prepared the brief speech. The piece of paper was in his pocket, and as he walked the few steps to the front of the stage he fingered it, wondering whether to take it out. No, he'd rather do it off the cuff but he knew that his Italian was not fluent. He began well, but faltered after a few sentences. He started again but got stuck. He looked agonisingly at the floor, blurted out a quiet, but audible 'shit', which the microphone picked up and sent round the room. The thousand guests responded with friendly laughter. The driver started again. At the end of the short address, his face was a little red.

At such moments, Michael would have liked the ground to swallow him up, or better, to disappear into the cockpit and behind a steering wheel, put his foot on the gas and drive off.

He had the same emotions at an event in Monza that season, out in the park surrounding the track, at an appearance for the fans organised by a sponsor. The drivers had been brought in to enliven the atmosphere — it is a routine part of their job, but it is also very stressful. As soon as the crowd began to get out of control, Michael tensed up. As he got out of the minibus, two bodyguards pushed him through a corridor of bodies, of screaming mouths and grasping hands. Luckily the organisers had made sure that it was not far to the stage. Rubens Barrichello was already up there. 'What do you think, Rubens?' the presenter shouted into his microphone. 'With all this support, you will be a second faster in the race the day after tomorrow?'

'At least!' Rubens replied, and the crowd roared. Then it was Michael's turn. The crowd roared again, even louder: the World Champion! At the end the presenter asked again whether support like this was worth about a second.

'Well,' answered Michael thoughtfully, 'you can't really say that. It's great of course to have all the support, but a whole second? To be honest, you really can't go along with that.' The final roar from the crowd is a bit less euphoric than the one afforded Rubens.

To have pandered to the presenter's understandable attempts at crowd pleasing wouldn't really have mattered, but it is something he can't do. It would be embarrassing, he would find it hypocritical. He never lies to journalists, even when they ask him questions he is not allowed to answer. Michael cleverly avoids giving a straight answer, or he laughs and asks whether the journalist really expects an answer. He once gave a wrong answer to a direct question at a press conference. Then at the press conference the next day, he seized the initiative and apologised for lying.

Only when he and Corinna are in control of the situation, among friends, and can try and make a photo-shoot fun, do they enjoy being photographed for the public's eyes. While in Texas Corinna and Michael had photos taken by Michel Comte out in the fields and ranches beyond Dallas.

'There were grasshoppers everywhere,' recalls Corinna. 'On us, in our hair and clothes, on our arms, legs, everywhere — terrible. The slightest movement and dozens of these little beasts suddenly leap in the air. But Michel Comte insisted that we lie and relax in the meadow. Like a lazy sunny afternoon. So Michael and I lazed around in the meadow, or at least we tried to. Not that grasshoppers are frightening, but really letting yourself hang loose was impossible. What's more, we kept on laughing when the creatures tried to jump into our mouths.

'And then Michel decided we should take the halters off the horses for the photos. It would look better, he said, more authentic, more natural. And so we were lying there in the meadow, the grasshoppers merrily jumping around on us, the horses next to us, happy that they were finally getting something to eat. The sun is blazing, the bees are gently humming, we are getting really sleepy. And suddenly one horse kicks the other full tilt in the chest with its hindquarters. But really hard, and several times. Just two metres away, Michael and I were lying on the ground as if we were relaxing. Honestly, it took about two seconds and we were on our feet and running.

'Michel had the most bizarre ideas of what we would do on this photo-shoot. He became sort of intoxicated with new ideas, most of which were unrealistic. We should, for instance, ride down the river, real cool and cowboy-like. Or we should roll around in the mud. Thanks very much! First of all, I thought it was a joke. But Michel was serious. Doing it at the drop of a hat felt just a little bit stupid and by the end, we were completely filthy, our faces, hair, fingernails, mud and dirt everywhere. Although I have to admit, as soon as we got over our inhibitions, was fun. Then I had to knock Michael over. Fine, nothing could be easier, could it? I eventually managed it, because we were both laughing so much. I did a few contorted Judo moves which made him practically fall over laughing anyway.

'We were on a ranch in Texas, just riding, and staying with a couple who breed quarter horses. Everything was very, very simple, and this was what made it so special. They put us up in a cabin with a little veranda at the front where we could all sit together in the evening. We felt really comfortable there, everything was so authentic and cosy, nothing fancy or pretentious.

'I thought it was fantastic of Michael to go along with this, and for us to have a riding holiday. It was something which I always wanted to do, but which he was not so keen on. But we complement each other and fit in with each other, each of us is interested in the other. We had, of course, been to the USA a few times before, mostly in Utah, and on Michael-type holidays, adventure things. I enjoyed these trips and took part in everything: driving quads, climbing, parachute jumping, things of that sort. This time I wanted to go to Texas and to see and ride these fantastic horses. Michael understands me. I understand him — that his passion is racing —and he understands me and my horses.'

At the go-kart track in Kerpen-Manheim is another of Michael's homes. Back in October 2001 it was cold and grey, with drizzling rain, gentle at first, then heavier. Puddles swimming with autumn leaves were forming on the unpaved road. People had their hoods pulled down and almost all had red caps peeping out. Tony Kart's green tent was at the back of the paddock. In front of it was a fence, and two security men ensured that only team members entered Tony Kart's little kingdom.

The site was heaving with people. They had all come for one person, and, because of the weather, they couldn't see him. The drivers had all crept off to one tent or another. Opposite the large tent was a smaller one. In it there was a long camping table and all down one side Raffaella had laid out a buffet. Plastic jugs with hot water, various sorts of tea bag, biscuits still in their packets, with sachets of sugar scattered among them. Of course there was an espresso machine — Tony Kart is an Italian team. Sitting on folding chairs at the table covered in plastic film, and clutching hot tea, were Michael and Corinna Schumacher and a few close friends. The women were wearing thick jackets and heavy boots and Michael's thin racing shoes had a protective plastic cover slipped over them. He was wearing a green racing overall and a green jacket — green is Tony Kart's colour, and it looked unusual on Michael — his angular jaw well in evidence. Two weeks before he had sealed his second winning World Championship season for Ferrari and on the weekend after he had been in Monza for the Ferrari celebration. Now he was in Kerpen-Manheim at the circuit where everything began for him. Although undoubtedly exhausted after the long season, he would never miss this very special go-kart race in his home town. It was the final round of the Super-A-World Championship, a serious business. Michael was roughly twice as old as the other participants, and because of a long life of sport he carried twice as much muscle as the young competitors. He had lost four kilos specially for this race and it showed, particularly in his face.

'In Formula One you need more muscle, which meant I was too heavy. On the first weigh-in we were nine kilos overweight. There's a limit of 140 kilos in go-karting and every excess kilo is a handicap. The Tony Kart team managed to build the go-kart 5 kilos lighter, and I had to do the rest. So I concentrated on losing muscle weight, and spent four hours a day on the bike, as opposed to the usual two, and we finally managed to get the scales down to 140.5 kilos.'

Having drunk his tea, Michael gave Corinna a kiss, and went across to the other tent. His race kart was up on the stocks, with a mechanic working on it. Michael grabbed a spanner and started removing the tank. Outside, through the mesh barrier, people were chanting his name, but Michael could no longer hear them. He was immersed in the world he loves so much. He was working on the vehicle and discussing with Signore Robazzi, the team boss, which tyres would be best suited for the rain. He had taken off his jacket, and was wearing just a waistcoat over his overall. His friend Peter Kaiser, for whose KSN-team Michael usually drives, joined them. This time, he was Michael's mechanic.

'I love working on go-karts. In Formula One you can't do anything yourself. All the mechanics are there to do the things which here you can do yourself. When Ralf was go-karting I was his mechanic, and I really loved it. This is my world, it is part of my natural rhythm, part of my childhood. Some of my happiest memories relate to this place and karting. I'm convinced that if I weren't a Formula One driver, I would be driving or hiring out go-karts. I certainly wouldn't have got rich doing it, but I would have been just as happy.'

Tonio Liuzzi from Italy won the World Championship. Michael was not in a position to have won the title because it was fought over ten races and he started in only the last two. But that isn't what it was about. 'I was really here just for the fun. For a long time I have wanted to take part again in a top-class, international go-kart race. And I must say, at the beginning, when it was dry, my times were really competitive. Funnily enough, in the wet I found it much more difficult, although that's usually my showpiece.' In the first of the two final runs Michael, who had started in 16th position, had to drop out when lying in third place because of a broken stub-axle bearing. In the first 400 meters he had moved up from sixteenth to fourth. In the second run, he moved up to third place, and was then awarded second because the winner, Marco Ardigo, was disqualified.

'I really love a duel, this wheel-to-wheel battling it out, all the overtaking manoeuvres and I get that here in abundance. I had to start in the middle of the field. It was tremendous fun, and a bit like old times. In go-karting, you can usually make up most of the places on the first lap." And late in the afternoon he sits in the damp tent with his wife and friends, pouring himself a weiss beer and revelling in the fresh memories of the last round of this go-kart World Championship. This had been Michael's first adult World Championship because when he was still active in the sport there hadn't been one for seniors.

Next day Michael could be found on a football pitch in Echichens, a little village in French-speaking Switzerland. A few of the team were already there. The changing room was in a little house and Michael was sitting on one of the long benches made of well-worn wood, doing up his boots. Patrick Ferrari, the trainer of the team which the Formula One World Champion plays for in his spare time, came in. In the third division of the Swiss amateur league, it was the same scene here as everywhere.

It was not just the club house which could do with a lick of paint. There was the sound of cow bells from the neighbouring meadow. Michael sometimes plays for the first team, sometimes for the second, sometimes for the veteran side. It all depends on his commitments and he is often away travelling. Patrick said something to the players which Michael only half understood. He doesn't speak French all that well. The players ran outside, with those typical short steps footballers take when running on paving stones in studs. Next to the little house a woman was waiting with her son: would it be possible to take a photo? Michael stood next to the child, a man in blue socks, white shirt, blue shorts, and smiled agreeably at the camera. The trainer looked on, impatiently. Michael ran his hand quickly over the boy's hair, pulled his socks up to his knees, then ran on to the pitch.

How much Michael loves playing football can best be ascertained by recalling how ill at ease he is on public occasions and when surrounded by crowds of people. Would he voluntarily submit himself to this stress if he weren't so keen? When Michael turns out for the Nazionale Piloti, a team in Italy made up of former or still active motor sportsmen, he is always the centre of attention. If it's announced he's playing, the stadium is sold out. If he can't, the opponents feel aggrieved, as do the town's grandees. For Michael, these games are always a matter of running the gauntlet. Before the match: how to get there, can he get right to the stadium by car, what entrance should he use? In the meanwhile: which dressing-room are the Piloti using — fathers with their sons are piling up there, good-looking women and journalists. And the argy-bargy begins: who knows someone who can get in? It's just a few autographs. Can someone look and see if Mikele is already there? Oh, he's getting a massage? Could he sign a few autographs at the same time? Can he come out of the changing-room early and give an interview? And a few autographs? Oh, he's due to give interviews outside? Won't it be too late by then? He has to leave straightaway? More appointments? Perhaps he can leave the pitch early, then he'll have time? As I was saying, just a few interviews, and while he is at it, he surely won't mind signing the flag, and the picture, and the running shoes. In these moments Michael slips through the crowds like he does on the track. Off through the middle.

'Football for me is a mixture of several things. On the one hand it's a welcome change from my daily training programme. It is simply a different form of exercise. And everyone knows this from their own experience, that you don't realise how much you are running when that ball is in play. On the other hand there is also the incentive that I am not very good at it. For example, when I go on to the pitch at Echichens for a game, I am sometimes more excited than when I get into my Formula One car. I also have to concentrate harder when receiving a pass than when I'm taking a corner, even if I am very quick about it. It is really odd: in a Formula One race I always have other capabilities in reserve when I am driving, but playing football, I have barely anything spare to see what's going on around me, and to string a really good passage of play together. As a child, like every other boy in Germany, I always wanted to play football, but I simply wasn't good enough and spent most of the time on the substitutes' bench. Now I am at least at the point where I can reasonably hold my own. Corinna sometimes has to laugh when — as sometimes happens — our weekend has to be organised round my games of football. When I am at home and can spare the time, I have to take advantage of it: then I play for several teams, one after the other.'

Training on Tuesdays, then out with the team for a pizza or a beer, and at the weekend a game off in a village somewhere. Leisure activity like that of thousands of fathers. Is that a first foretaste of life in retirement for Schumacher the Formula One driver? Who knows. Michael himself has no idea what will happen after he has finished and he doesn't want to get too preoccupied with it either. He once spoke in an interview of wanting to become the 'TT' when his racing career was over, the 'Turniertrottel' (tournament dogsbody) for Corinna. After all, his wife has organised her whole life round him, and he would now reverse the situation and accompany her to her riding events, muck out the stables, and do all those little jobs which would make him her 'TT'. He said this with a smile, but a smile doesn't get into print. The word 'TT' was taken up enthusiastically worldwide, distributed on countless internet pages, without anyone abroad having the remotest idea what it meant. But it was the first time that Michael had said what he was going to do at the end of his career — a genuine news item: *Michael Schumacher has revealed for the first time that after his racing career he will become a 'TT'.*

As usual, the irony in his words somehow got lost on the journey round the globe. 'TT' was just a symbol for 'no idea'. The end of Michael's career is too far off, it doesn't yet figure in his plans. Why should it? If he has learnt anything in a lifetime as a sportsman, it is that you have to take it one step at a time, and mustn't look too far ahead. Otherwise you lose sight of what lies in the immediate present.

For many observers, this attitude is hard to follow. They experience the goal-oriented Schumacher, the one who always knows exactly what he wants, and how he can achieve it. The one who has firm ideas and firm principles. Just to live for the day, with no goal or plan, that, they think, doesn't fit with this man.

But Michael knows the meaning of laissez-faire. 'Just to live for the day, to wait and see what each day brings, I could imagine that could be exciting for a while. When I finally give up, at first I will do nothing at all. I am already looking forward to having no appointments, and not having the whole year planned out for me. I could well understand Mika Häkkinen when he retired and said it was good to get away from the grind. I would like to enjoy the luxury of taking things as they come. I don't want to know in February everything I have to do in May, I want to get rid of the rhythm of the racing calendar. And sooner or later the roof will fall in on me. I'm sure something interesting will turn up but I don't yet want to be bothered with thinking what it will be. Not consciously at least, for if I did, my head wouldn't be 100 per cent focused on racing. And that wouldn't be me.'

Some time ago, the graphologist Andreas Franz analysed Michael's signature for the *Frankfurter Rundschau*, and came to the following conclusions:

'The first letter in Michael's signature already looks like a race track. The racing driver begins the "M" with a long upwards stroke, which ends in a curve. The handwriting resembles a straight, ending in a hairpin corner. The speed of the writing on the paper, also recognisable in "Schumacher", reveals the Formula One Champion's quickness of thought. He can put plans swiftly into practice, and is flexible. The sharp upper part of the "M" which leans strongly to the left, demonstrates willingness to take risks. He does, however, know his limitations, and is not prepared to go beyond these for the sake of success. Although he is the most successful driver of all time, his initial emphasis is not exaggerated. This demonstrates that Schumacher is perfectly aware of his public recognition, but is not particularly impressed by fame and attention. The illegibility of the letters reveals that he is wary of showing his cards. He is always thinking up tricks to catch his rivals by surprise. The inclination towards the right proves that only the future interests him, the past plays a subordinate role. What is also striking is that his signature is thickish, rather than thin, which characterises him as a man of human warmth and generosity. A further indication of this are the large loops. He is an artist of a different kind, one who has mastery of a car second to none, but who has never lost sight of the essentials — his wife and his children. Perhaps that is his recipe for success.'

Perhaps the man is right.

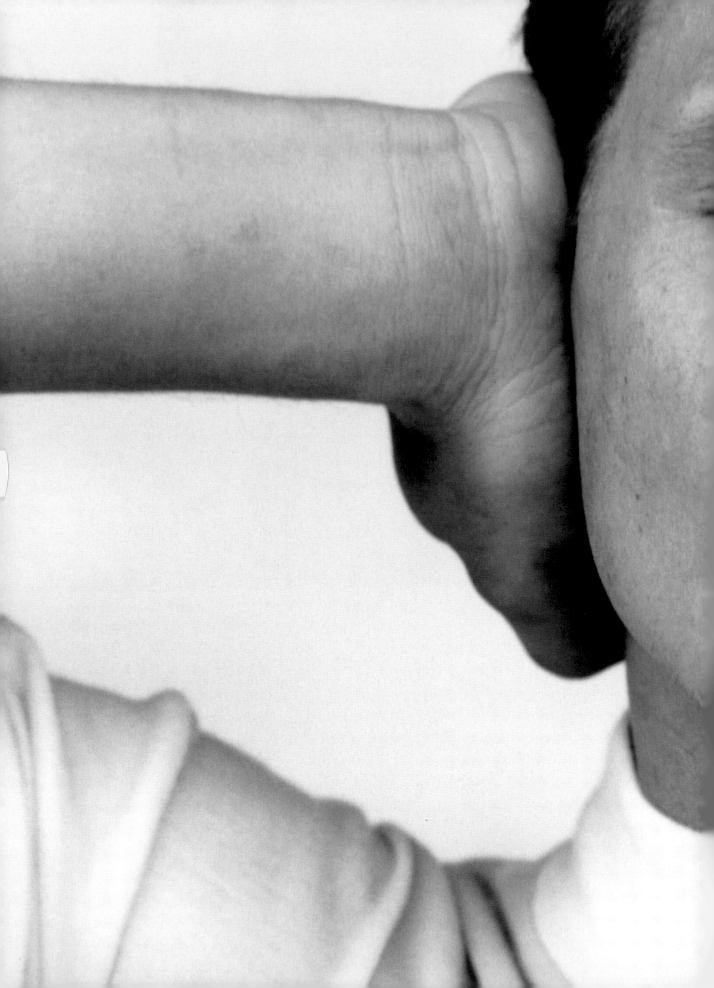

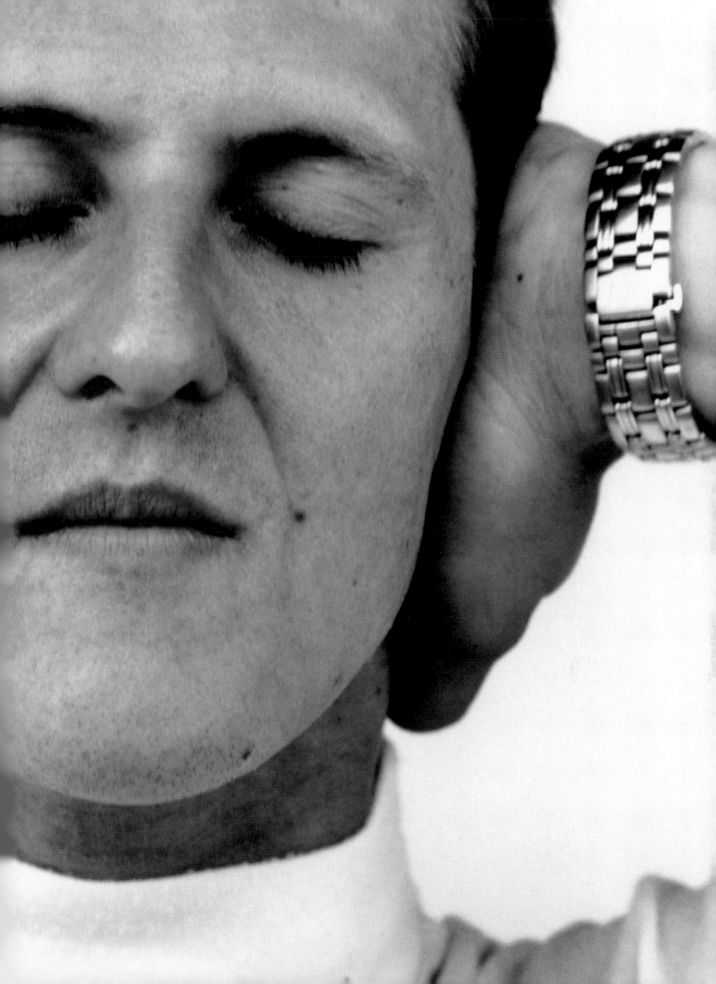

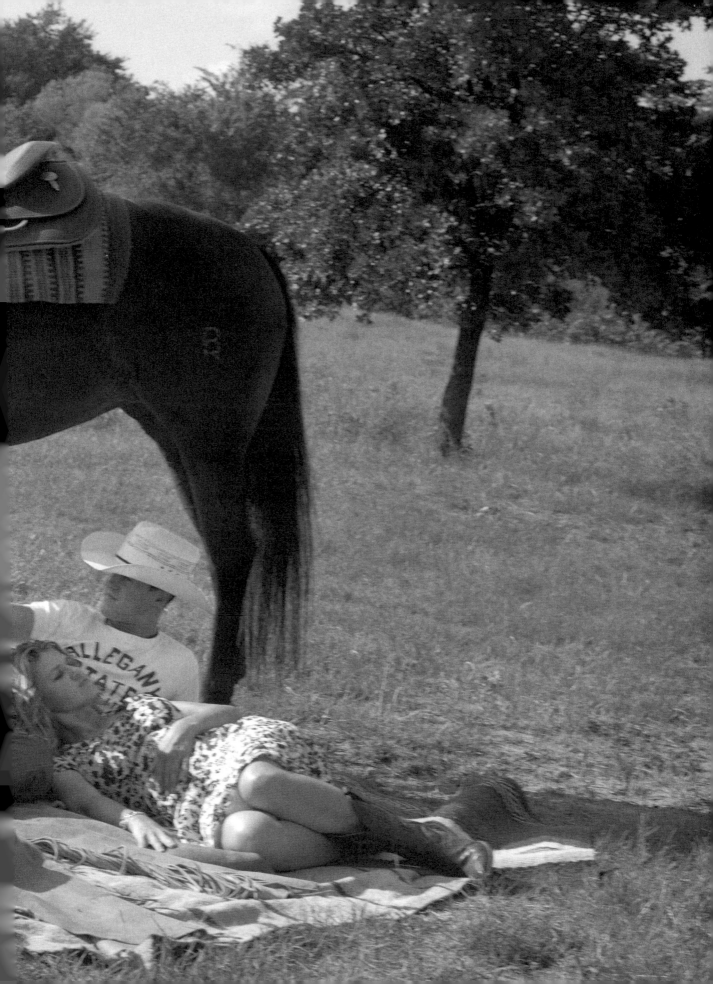

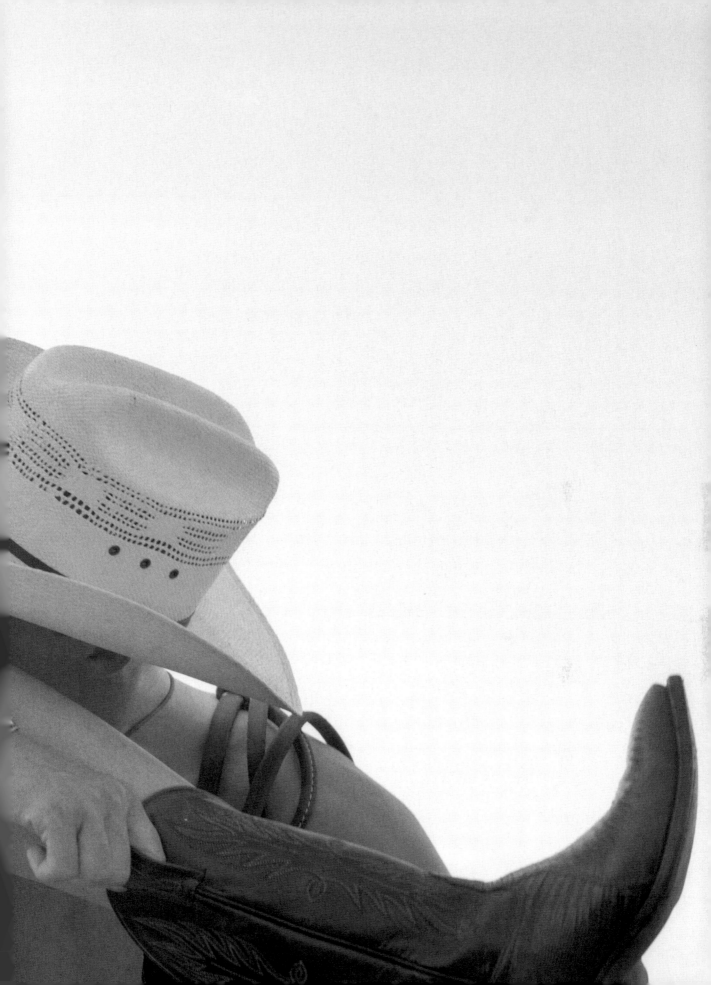

GENERAL

The yellow flags were not waved to instruct to slow down before any turn 12 and turn the circu...
session and marshall. Now marshals for extra yellow practice and several drivers ig...
wave yellow flags to ... show down extra Friday practice to clean the circu...
turn 2 — The same must be shown and not work, and several Friday practice to clean the...
straight when flags are shown the appreciate the first...
session)

Furthermore the blue flags are particularly dirty during, we weekend.
too long to give the way. In the the GP weekend.

Finally, the track was particularly dirty during the banking.
drivers suffered of punctures before in the GP weekend.
with the appropriate machine to the banking.

TURN 11

Tarmac is needed in turn 11 at 1...
to resurface correctly by following...

Telefax: +377 92 05 79 36

...6NX

le Coronado • 20. Avenu...

Regist...

Michael Schumacher: Career Statistics

As at the end of the 2002 season.

World Championships
1st   Juan Manuel Fangio (Argentina) and Michael Schumacher (Germany), both 5
3rd   Alain Prost (France) 4

Grand Prix Victories
1st   Michael Schumacher 64
2nd   Alain Prost 51
3rd   Ayrton Senna (Brazil) 41

Victories in one Season
1st   Michael Schumacher 11 (2002)
2nd   Nigel Mansell (GB/1992) and Michael Schumacher (1995, 2000, 2001), both 9

Podium Finishes
1st   Michael Schumacher 114
2nd   Prost 106

Pole Positions
1st   Senna 65
2nd   Michael Schumacher 50
3rd   Jim Clark (GB) and Prost, both 33

World Championship Points
1st   Michael Schumacher 945
2nd   Prost 798.5
3rd   Senna 614

Points in one Season
1st   Michael Schumacher 144 (2002)
2nd   Michael Schumacher 123 (2001)
3rd   Mansell (1992) and Michael Schumacher (2000), both 108

Largest Gap between World Champion and Second Place in Final Standings
1st   Michael Schumacher 67 (2002)
2nd   Michael Schumacher 58 (2001)
3rd   Mansell 52 (1992)

Fastest World Champion
1st   Michael Schumacher (2002) after 11 out of 17 races (64,71 %)
2nd   Mansell (1992) after 11 out of 16 (68,75 %)
3rd   Clark (1963 und 1965) after 7 out of 10 (70 %)

Fastest laps
1st   Michael Schumacher 51
2nd   Prost 41
3rd   Mansell 30

2002

Scuderia Ferrari Marlboro   **Ferrari F1-2002 051 V10**

Grand Prix	Circuit	Date	Grid	Time	Result	Comments
Australia	Albert Park	3 Mar	2nd	1:35:36.792	1st	
Malaysia	Sepang	17 Mar	Pole	1:35:14.707	3rd	
Brazil	Interlagos	31 Mar	2nd	1:31:43.662	1st	
San Marino	Imola	14 Apr	Pole	1:29:10.789	1st	
Spain	Barcelona	28 Apr	Pole	1:30:29.981	1st	Fastest Lap
Austria	A1 Ring	12 May	3rd	1:33:51.562	1st	Fastest Lap
Monaco	Monte Carlo	26 May	3rd	1:45:40.105	2nd	
Canada	Montreal	9 Jun	2nd	1:33:39.055	1st	
European	Nürburgring	23 Jun	2nd	1:35:07.720	2nd	Fastest Lap
Great Britain	Silverstone	7 Jul	3rd	1:31:45.015	1st	
France	Magny Cours	21 Jul	2nd	1:32:09.837	1st	
Germany	Hockenheim	28 Jul	Pole	1:27:52.078	1st	Fastest Lap
Hungary	Hungaroring	18 Aug	2nd	1:41:49.435	2nd	Fastest Lap
Belgium	Spa	1 Sep	Pole	1:21:20.634	1st	Fastest Lap
Italy	Monza	15 Sep	2nd	1:16:22.237	2nd	
USA	Indianapolis	29 Sep	Pole	1:31:07.945	2nd	
Japan	Suzuka	13 Oct	Pole	1:26:59.698	1st	Fastest Lap

Summary of Year

Pole Positions	7
Fastest Laps	7
Grand Prix Wins	11
Podium Finishes	17
Total Points	144
World Championship Position	1st

2001

Scuderia Ferrari Marlboro   **Ferrari F1-2001 050 V10**

Grand Prix	Circuit	Date	Grid	Time	Result	Comments
Australia	Albert Park	4 Mar	Pole	1:38:26.533	1st	Fastest Lap
Malaysia	Sepang	18 Mar	Pole	1:47:34.801	1st	
Brazil	Interlagos	1 Apr	Pole	1:39:16.998	2nd	
San Marino	Imola	15 Apr	4th	-	Rtd.	Mechanical failure. Lap 24
Spain	Barcelona	29 Apr	Pole	1:31:03.305	1st	Fastest Lap
Austria	A1 Ring	13 May	Pole	1:27:48.118	2nd	
Monaco	Monte Carlo	27 May	2nd	1:47:22.561	1st	
Canada	Montreal	10 Jun	Pole	1:34:51.757	2nd	
Europe	Nürburgring	24 Jun	Pole	1:29:42.724	1st	
France	Magny Cours	1 Jul	2nd	1:33:35.636	1st	
Great Britain	Silverstone	15 Jul	Pole	1:25:67.416	2nd	
Germany	Hockenheim	29 Jul	4th	-	Rtd.	Fuel pressure. Lap 23
Hungary	Hungaroring	19 Aug	Pole	1:41:49.675	1st	
Belgium	Spa	2 Sep	3rd	1:08:05.002	1st	Fastest Lap
Italy	Monza	16 Sep	3rd	1:16:83.484	4th	
USA	Indianapolis	30 Sep	Pole	1:32:53.886	2nd	
Japan	Suzuka	14 Oct	Pole	1:27:33.298	1st	

Summary of Year

Pole Positions	11
Fastest Laps	3
Grand Prix Wins	9
Podium Finishes	14
Total Points	123
World Championship Position	1st

2000

Scuderia Ferrari Marlboro   **Ferrari F1-2000 049 V10**

Grand Prix	Circuit	Date	Grid	Time	Result	Comments
Australia	Melbourne	12 Mar	3rd	1:34:01.987	1st	
Brazil	Interlagos	26 Mar	3rd	1:31:35.271	1st	Fastest Lap
San Marino	Imola	9 Apr	2nd	1:31:39.776	1st	
Great Britain	Silverstone	23 Apr	5th	1:28:70.025	3rd	
Spain	Barcelona	7 May	Pole	1:34:03.373	5th	
Europe	Nurburgring	21 May	2nd	1:42:00.307	1st	Fastest Lap
Monaco	Monte Carlo	4 Jun	Pole	-	Rtd.	Broken exhaust. Lap 55
Canada	Montreal	18 Jun	Pole	1:41:12.313	1st	
France	Magny Cours	2 Jul	Pole	-	Rtd.	Engine failure. Lap 58
Austria	A1 Ring	16 Jul	4th	-	Rtd.	Accident. Lap 1
Germany	Hockenheim	30 Jul	2nd	-	Rtd.	Accident with Fisichella. Lap 1
Hungary	Hungaroring	13 Aug	Pole	1:45:41.785	2nd	
Belgium	Spa	27 Aug	4th	1:28:15.597	2nd	
Italy	Monza	10 Sep	Pole	1:27:31.638	1st	
USA	Indianapolis	24 Sep	Pole	1:36:30.883	1st	
Japan	Suzuka	8 Oct	Pole	1:29:53.435	1st	
Malaysia	Sepang	22 Oct	Pole	1:35:54.235	1st	

Summary of Year

Pole Positions	9
Fastest Laps	2
Grand Prix Wins	9
Podium Finishes	12
Total Points	108
World Championship Position	1st

1999

Scuderia Ferrari Marlboro   **Ferrari 399 048 V10**

Grand Prix	Circuit	Date	Grid	Time	Result	Comments
Australia	Melbourne	7 Mar	3rd	-	8th	Fastest Lap. Puncture Lap 31
Brazil	Interlagos	11 Apr	4th	1:36:08.710	2nd	
San Marino	Imola	2 May	3rd	1:33:44.792	1st	Fastest Lap
Monaco	Monte Carlo	16 May	2nd	1:49:31.812	1st	
Spain	Barcelona	30 May	4th	1:34:24.510	3rd	Fastest Lap
Canada	Montreal	13 Jun	Pole	-	Rtd.	Accident Lap 29
France	Magny Cours	28 Jun	6th	1:58:72.224	5th	
Britain	Silverstone	11 Jul	2nd	-	Rtd.	Accident at start
Austria	A1 Ring	25 Jul	Did not enter	-	-	Injured
Germany	Hockenheim	1 Aug	Did not enter	-	-	Injured
Hungary	Hungaroring	15 Aug	Did not enter	-	-	Injured
Belgium	Spa	29 Aug	Did not enter	-	-	Injured
Italy	Monza	12 Sep	Did not enter	-	-	Injured
Europe	Nürburgring	26 Sep	Did not enter	-	-	Injured
Malaysia	Sepang	17 Oct	Pole	1:36:39.534	2nd	Fastest Lap
Japan	Suzuka	31 Oct	Pole	1:31:23.800	2nd	Fastest Lap

Summary of Year

Pole Positions	3
Fastest Laps	5
Grand Prix Wins	2
Podium Finishes	6
Total Points	44
World Championship Position	5th

1998

Scuderia Ferrari Marlboro   Ferrari 300 047 V10

Grand Prix	Circuit	Date	Grid	Time	Result	Comments
Australia	Melbourne	8 Mar	3rd	-	Rtd.	Engine Lap 5
Brazil	Ingerlagos	29 Mar	4th	1:38:12.297	3rd	
Argentina	Buenos Aires	12 Apr	2nd	1:48:36.175	1st	
San Marino	Imola	26 Apr	3rd	1:34:29.147	2nd	Fastest Lap
Spain	Barcelona	10 May	3rd	1:34:24.716	3rd	
Monaco	Monte Carlo	24 May	4th	-	10th	Accident with Wurz. Lap 37
Canada	Montreal	7 Jun	3rd	1:40:57.355	1st	Fastest Lap
France	Magny Cours	28 Jun	2nd	1:34:45.026	1st	
Britain	Silverstone	12 Jul	2nd	1:47:02.450	1st	Fastest Lap
Austria	A1 Ring	26 Jul	4th	1:30:83.179	3rd	
Germany	Hockenheim	2 Aug	3rd	1:21:00.597	5th	
Hungary	Hungaroring	16 Aug	3rd	1:45:25.550	1st	Fastest Lap
Belgium	Spa	30 Aug	4th	-	Rtd.	Fastest Lap. Accident with Coulthard
Italy	Monza	13 Sep	Pole	1:17:09.672	1st	
Europe	Nürburgring	27 Sep	Pole	1:32:17.001	2nd	
Japan	Suzuka	1 Nov	Pole	-	Rtd.	Fastest Lap. Tyre exploded. Lap 31

Summary of Year

Pole Positions	3
Fastest Laps	6
Grand Prix Wins	6
Podium Finishes	11
Total Points	86
World Championship Position	2nd

1997

Scuderia Ferrari Marlboro   Ferrari 310B 046 V10
Ferrari 310B 046/2 V10

Grand Prix	Circuit	Date	Grid	Time	Result	Comments
Australia	Melbourne	9 Mar	3rd	1:30:48.764	2nd	
Brazil	Interlagos	30 Mar	4th	1:36:40.721	5th	
Argentina	Buenos Aires	13 Apr	4th	-	Rtd.	Accident at start
San Marino	Imola	27 Apr	3rd	1:31:01.910	2nd	
Monaco	Monte Carlo	11 May	2nd	2:00:05.654	1st	Fastest Lap
Spain	Barcelona	25 May	7th	1:30:53.875	4th	
Canada	Montreal	15 Jun	Pole	1:17:40.616	1st	
France	Magny Cours	29 Jun	Pole	1:38:50.492	1st	Fastest Lap
Britain	Silverstone	13 Jul	4th	-	Rtd.	Fastest Lap. Wheel bearing Lap 38
Germany	Hockenheim	27 Jul	4th	1:20:76.573	2nd	
Hungary	Hungaroring	10 Aug	Pole	1:45:77.650	4th	
Belgium	Spa	24 Aug	3rd	1:33:46.717	1st	
Italy	Monza	7 Sep	9th	1:17:16.090	6th	
Austria	A1 Ring	21 Sep	9th	1:27:69.410	6th	
Luxembourg	Nürburgring	28 Sep	5th	-	Rtd.	Accident with Ralf Schumacher Lap 2
Japan	Suzuka	12 Oct	2nd	1:29:48.446	1st	
Europe	Jerez	26 Oct	2nd	-	Rtd.	Accident with Villeneuve Lap 47

Summary of Year

Pole Positions	3
Fastest Laps	3
Grand Prix Wins	5
Podium Finishes	8
Total Points	(78)
World Championship Position	(2nd) Excluded by the F.I.A.

1996

Scuderia Ferrari   Ferrari 310 046 V10

Grand Prix	Circuit	Date	Grid	Time	Result	Comments
Australia	Melbourne	10 Mar	4th	-	Rtd.	Brake fluid loss. Lap 32
Brazil	Interlagos	31 Mar	4th	70 of 71 laps	3rd	
Argentina	Buenos Aires	7 Apr	2nd	-	Rtd.	Rear wing. Lap 46
Europe	Nürburgring	28 Apr	3rd	1:33:27.235	2nd	
San Marino	Imola	5 May	Pole	1:35:42.616	2nd	
Monaco	Monte Carlo	19 May	Pole	-	Rtd.	Accident at start
Spain	Barcelona	2 Jun	3rd	1:59:49.307	1st	Fastest Lap
Canada	Montreal	16 Jun	3rd	-	Rtd.	Drive shaft. Lap 41
France	Magny Cours	30 Jun	Pole	-	Rtd.	Engine parade lap
Britain	Silverstone	14 Jul	3rd	-	Rtd.	Hydraulics Lap 3
Germany	Hockenheim	28 Jul	3rd	1:22:24.934	4th	
Hungary	Hungaroring	11 Aug	Pole	-	Rtd.	Throttle control unit. Lap 70
Belgium	Spa	25 Aug	3rd	1:28:15.125	1st	
Italy	Monza	8 Sep	3rd	1:17:43.632	1st	Fastest lap
Portugal	Estoril	22 Sep	4th	1:41:16.680	3rd	
Japan	Suzuka	13 Oct	3rd	1:32:35.674	2nd	

Summary of Year

Pole Positions	4
Fastest Laps	2
Grand Prix Wins	3
Podium Finishes	8
Total Points	59
World Championship Position	3rd

1995

Mild Seven Benetton Ford   3.0 Benetton B195 - Renault V10

Grand Prix	Circuit	Date	Grid	Time	Result	Comments
Brazil	Interlagos	26 Mar	2nd	1:38:34.154	1st	
Argentina	Buenos Aires	9 Apr	3rd	1:53:47.908	3rd	
San Marino	Imola	30 Apr	Pole	-	Rtd.	Accident Lap 10
Spain	Barcelona	14 May	Pole	1:34:20.507	1st	
Monaco	Monte Carlo	28 May	2nd	1:53:11.258	1st	
Canada	Montreal	11 Jun	Pole	1:47:08.393	5th	
France	Magny Cours	2 Jul	2nd	1:38:28.429	1st	
Britain	Silverstone	16 Jul	2nd	-	Rtd.	Accident with Hill.Lap 45
Germany	Hockenheim	30 Jul	2nd	1:22:56.043	1st	
Hungary	Hungaroring	13 Aug	3rd	-	11th	Fuel pump. Lap 73
Belgium	Spa	27 Aug	16th	1:36:47.875	1st	
Italy	Monza	10 Sep	2nd	-	Rtd.	Accident with Hill. Lap 23
Portugal	Estoril	24 Sep	3rd	1:41:59.393	2nd	
Europe	Nürburgring	1 Oct	3rd	1:39:50.044	1st	
Pacific	Aida	22 Oct	2nd	1:48:49.972	1st	
Japan	Suzuka	29 Oct	Pole	1:36:52.930	1st	
Australia	Adelaide	12 Nov	3rd	-	Rtd.	Accident with Alesi. Lap 25

Summary of Year

Pole Positions	4
Fastest Laps	8
Grand Prix Wins	8
Podium Finishes	10
Total Points	102
World Championship Position	1st

Photographs taken at:

Silverstone July 1996
Barcelona April 1998
Antibes May 1999
Lausanne January 2001
Maranello April 2002
Texas June 2002
Maranello July 2002

With thanks to Willi Weber, Jean Todt, Scuderia Ferrari, Stern, Max, Fila, Daniela König, Sue Tsai, Bruno Macor, Jérôme Navarre, Eddie Adams, Heiner Buchinger, Jörg Hunke, Elmar Brümmer, Frank Quednau.

First Edition 2003

10 9 8 7 6 5 4 3 2 1

Published by Ebury Press
Photographs © Michel Comte
Text © Sabine Kehm
Copyright for this edition Steidl

Project produced by Lucas Albers
Edited by Michael Mack and Gerhard Steidl
Book design by Michael Mack and Steidl Design

Scans done at Steidl's digital darkroom

ISBN 0-091894-352

First published in Great Britain in 2003 by Ebury Press
Random House, 20 Vauxhall Bridge Road, London SW1V 2SA

Random House Australia (Pty) Limited, 20 Alfred Street,
Milsons Point, Sydney, New South Wales 2061, Australia

Random House New Zealand Limited, 18 Poland Road,
Glenfield, Auckland 10, New Zealand

Random House (Pty) Limited, Endulini, 5A Jubilee Road,
Parktown 2193, South Africa

The Random House Group Limited Reg. No. 954009
www.randomhouse.co.uk

A CIP catalogue record for this book
is available from the British Library

Printed and bound in Germany
by Appl, Wemding

Papers used by Ebury Press are natural, recyclable products
made from wood grown in sustainable forests.